WHAT PEOPLE ARE SAYING ABOUT THIS BOOK:

"*Beyond Your Limits* is a powerful testament to the results of resilience and focused goal-setting. The blend of practical advice with the seven-step framework, and personal reflection overcoming adversity, makes this book a must-read for anyone looking to grow radically and achieve more than they ever thought possible."

- **Dr. Marshall Goldsmith** is the *Thinkers50* #1 Executive Coach and New York Times bestselling author of *The Earned Life*, *Triggers*, and *What Got You Here Won't Get You There*.

"There are many comments I could make about Pramoda's *Beyond Your Limits* but the one I will focus on is something I have learned in life about choosing a goal and staying inspired. I have found one consistent ingredient in all of the goals I have chosen and accomplished. That ingredient is a mentor who not only gave me the physical and mental mechanics necessary to accomplish the goal but they gave me proof in their method by demonstrating they possessed the skill I would need and wanted in order to reach my goal. For me this is the foundation of success because it immediately inspires action and creates stamina during the process. My jazz piano teacher didn't just tell me what to practice, he SHOWED what it would sound like to execute the skill.

My golf instructor didn't just say "swing this way" he showed me how those mechanics enabled him to hit a brilliant shot. Pramoda's honesty and one might even say vulnerability to share his inner thoughts and emotion on his journey to personal power is a gift for all who read his work."

    - **Thomas M. Sterne**r Author of *The Practicing Mind, Fully Engaged and It's Just A Thought.*

"In his new book, *Beyond Your Limits*, Pramoda Vyasarao offers contemporary wisdom that is immediately actionable in our technology-fueled life. His journey takes us from the Israeli martial art of Krav Maga, through the magic of reading the Kamasutra in Sanskrit, to becoming a 'Spartan.' Surprisingly easy and enjoyable to read, the book is yet full of thoughtfulness that will keep you thinking long after you've finished it."

    - **Bence Gazdag**, Vice President at Oracle

"Even after having read tens of books on goals, *Beyond Your Limits* gave me a fresh lens to approach my life through goals. If you don't want a boring life, get this book."

    - **Krishna Kiran**, Co-founder and CEO at Profile.
    fyi, Ex-Amazon Head of Engineering

"*Beyond Your Limits* reveals the inspiring story and practical wisdom of my friend and coach, Pramoda, who is a master at achieving goals. The moment I finished reading, I wrote down 52 of my own goals spanning family, work, and fitness. The book's 7-step framework has become my go-to guide for making them happen. It's a must-read for anyone serious about reaching their potential."

    - **Nassar Stoertz**, Start-up Founder and Staff Engineer at Google

"This narrative isn't merely instructive; it's an invitation from someone who's navigated life's ups and downs with resilience and intention. *Beyond Your Limits* is a guide for anyone looking to enrich their journey."

  - **Srikanthan Kumarasamy**, Co-Founder at Guiding Light Coaching Services

"The way Pramoda decimated a goal list that would have challenged even the most effective elite athletes is inspiring. I'm glad that he has written about his trials and tribulations. Pramoda has shared his best hacks so that more people may be inspired to set Everest-level goals. *Beyond Your Limits* will motivate and persuade readers to want to be more and do more!"

  - **Ian Faria**, Leadership Facilitator and Mind Coach

"Pramoda takes us on a captivating and inspirational journey in *Beyond the Limits*. He displays remarkable self-awareness about his shortcomings and how he grew through goals. He shows how his life transformed by setting and achieving goals—from questioning the purpose of his life to now helping others achieve their goals and finding fulfillment. I have now set goals that I want to achieve."

  - **Umang Vanjara**, Head of Platform at Taulia

"Each chapter in this book is an easy read and can be read in any order. Every reflective question needs you to deeply introspect and elevate your thinking to a higher level, to better yourself and the world around you."

  - **Santosh Vijay**, CTO, Leadership and Career Coach

BEYOND YOUR LIMITS

The Proven Path For Achieving Growth, Happiness, And Meaning With Expansive Goals

PRAMODA VYASARAO

ISBN: 979-8-89316-234-9 - paperback

ISBN: 979-8-89316-235-6 - ebook

ISBN: 979-8-89316-322-3 - hardcover

ISBN: 979-8-89316-324-7 - audiobook

DOWNLOAD THE BEYOND YOUR LIMITS WORKBOOK FREE

READ THIS FIRST

To make reflecting on your goals easier, I would like to offer this workbook as your companion.

You can download the workbook using the link below:
changesmith.me/workbook

DEDICATION

Appa: the foundation of belief in my life
Amma: the light of my life
Anusha: the love of my life
Samyak: the joy of my life

My Father

"When I was young, I spent a lot of time with my father, strengthening our bond by going for walks and swimming. However, when we moved to America, the environment and the people were new—and for a four-year-old, that was scary. I hadn't met many people outside my own family before, so my reaction was quite genuine: I was scared, yet I was also enjoying America because our family had a warrior, my father. He stayed by our side and led us into our new lives. I knew this because of a fundamental lesson I learned from him: You don't need to fight in wars to earn the title of a warrior; you can be a warrior for many reasons, such as standing up for yourself and others, and working hard. After all, without pressure, there are no diamonds. These are all attributes of a warrior, whose best weapon is their *mind. He led by example, doing all that he did for us. But that wasn't all. He showed me what it means to be a true warrior of the mind. So now, I strive to be that kind of warrior." - Samyak*

TABLE OF CONTENTS

FOREWORD

I t is hard to imagine that a book about setting goals and living a life oriented around goals could have anything new to say. Every coach is taught to organize his or her coaching around goal-setting and goal-monitoring and the idea of the importance of goals is embedded in our contemporary way of living. Goals, goals, goals! Talk of goals is everywhere.

And so, it is remarkable that Pramoda Vyasarao's new book *Beyond Your Limits* should feel so fresh, original, and valuable. I think that the book moves us because the author is sharing so authentically. He communicates his fear of drowning, his unhappiness with his weight, his desire to be of use by giving blood, and his other deepest thoughts, feelings, and ambitions in a way that touches us and that makes us want to live just as authentically.

In this context, goals do not feel like disembodied "shoulds" that are created as one creates a grocery shopping list. They are seen to flow from the grand existential task of living the project of one's life on one's own terms. A goal is chosen because it defeats a fear, because it connects to a deep yearning, because it flows from a cherished value. This is the essence of existential goal-setting!

The author communicates how goals connect to our deepest reasons for being. If we want to make ourselves proud, he argues convincingly, then that intention will naturally lead us to set goals aligned with that intention. There is a certain simple calculus involved here: want to make yourself proud? Set goals and achieve them!

Like the author of any useful self-help book, Pramoda provides the reader with a simple, useful framework for setting goals and achieving goals. He identifies and describes seven steps—begin with the end in mind, become accountable, define milestones, take one day at a time, bounce back, quit strategically, and enjoy the journey—and we nod, because we see how he has lived them.

Because he shares with us his lived journey, we see how the roadmap that these steps represent has arisen from true life experience. We do not need footnotes, quotes from gurus, or references. It is plain as day, why these steps are the steps to follow. I hope that you'll enjoy this book as much as I did and that you'll find it genuinely valuable. I believe that you will!

Dr. Eric Maisel
Creativity Coach and author of 60 books

A Note to the Reader

This book doesn't offer information. It's the era of information indigestion. There's abundant information on the internet. You are one search or one-sentence prompt away from pages of curated knowledge.

I won't attempt to add a bucketful to the ocean of knowledge freely available to us. Instead, what the world needs is a demonstration—a demonstration of a personal vision, clear goals, and consistent action toward those goals. We need a personal example. That's where this book can help—serving as the bridge from information to inspired action. A bridge from information to *implementation*!

My objective is to provide a demonstration of applying our knowledge toward life goals and, through my example, light the fire of inspiration in your mind.

This book is a conversation between you and me. I recommend reading this book in the order I present it, divided into three sections. Start with the first section and then read the other two. You can always come back and reread portions of the book for sustained inspiration in the future.

I sincerely hope this book will start your journey of personal transformation through goals.

If this book inspires you to write one goal and achieve that goal in the next one to three years, the book has served its purpose. My effort on this book has not been in vain.

INTRODUCTION

When I was twenty-two, my father passed away. At the time I was working toward getting my master's degree in computer science and had a job offer from Oracle to join them right after graduation. My father was super proud of me. I fondly remember when he showed my offer letter and compensation details to his friends. My salary was more than what he was earning after thirty years of working as a teacher, so I understood his excitement.

Academics were my central focus for six years, from 1996 to 2002. Everything else was non-existent. There was no life beyond my studies. Seeing my parents so proud of my academic achievements was a primary motivator for my hard work. My father's belief and pride in me was the foundation of my self-belief.

His sudden death in January 2001 created a void in me. I started asking questions about the meaning of life, the purpose of our existence, and what it might really mean to live a life of happiness and fulfillment.

This pain and inquiry simmered for several months. A year after my father's passing, I joined Oracle as a software engineer, and life became busy. I lived in Bengaluru, India. On the outside, I had a high-paying job, attractive perks, access to free food in the cafeteria, and a club membership. On the inside, I felt empty and life was meaningless.

These existential inquiries continued surfacing in my mind on weekends when I often found myself not fully engaged in any particular activity. I found solace in self-help books and I read them as a cathartic outlet. Before finishing a book, I ordered those recommended by the author, driven by my craving for more information. At this time, I weighed 82 kilograms (180 pounds). I had gained 5 kilograms in one year. It was trending upward due to a sedentary lifestyle. I didn't find physical activity enjoyable. I was wrapped in my thoughts most of the time, thinking about my thinking and analyzing my feelings. I was engrossed in the never-ending movie of my mind.

I had an opportunity to travel to the US for three months in December 2002. Ninety days of living alone in an apartment allowed me to reflect a lot on my lifestyle, habits, and behaviors. It was all limited to thinking; I didn't change anything in my choices. My lifestyle continued to be sedentary and I put on more weight by continually eating while watching TV. I binge-watched action movies in hopes of injecting some thrill into my otherwise dull life. I weighed 89 kilograms (196 pounds) and looked like a beanbag. All the action took place in the movies, not in my life.

During my stay in the US, my grandfather passed away—exactly two years after my father's passing. Mobile phones were not easily accessible in those days, so it took three days before I was notified; they had to call my work number to reach me. I was his favorite grandson, yet I wasn't there to witness his last rites.

My grandfather's death intensified the pain. My mind was filled with the same questions as before: What's the meaning of life? Why do we live? What are we supposed to do while we're alive?

I was still enjoying basking in self-help books when I went back to India three months later. Without much application, all the inspiration was rotting. I thought I had a challenge with time management. At the time, I felt that my life would improve if only I knew how to manage time. I signed up for a two-day course on time management offered at Oracle. The facilitator was an accountant turned soft-skills trainer.

During the training, he talked about a man named John Goddard. John's story shook me to the core. At age 15, he listed 127[1] goals on paper—he called it My Life List. John's list included exploring numerous countries, climbing major mountains, running a mile in under five minutes, and solo piloting a plane around the world, among many others. By 2003, he had achieved most of them. Many of his goals needed dedication, effort, and deliberate practice.

Inspired by his true story, I wrote my own life list. I didn't have crazy goals like climbing the world's highest mountains; I didn't have an interest in them. Instead, I wrote ordinary goals. Goals that would fulfill me. Goals that would help me live a life without regret. I wrote these five goals on my list that day. I have added details on the rationale behind these goals below.

1. Lose 15 kilograms (33 pounds). I weighed 89 kilograms (or 196 pounds), my waistline measured 38 inches, and I wore extra-large clothes to hide my love handles. I wanted to reach my ideal weight.
2. Learn to swim. I was afraid of water and I wanted to overcome this fear.
3. Become a confident public speaker. I was terrified of speaking in public. It showed in workplace meetings. I mumbled and fumbled in front of a group. I didn't like it.
4. Learn one form of martial arts. I liked Bruce Lee and Jackie Chan in my teenage years. I wanted to learn Karate. This dream hadn't materialized; now I had a second chance as an adult, so I wrote it on the list.

---

1   https://www.johngoddard.info/

5. Donate blood 50 times. I had donated six times before writing this goal. I knew the value of blood donation through a family member's experience. I wanted to continue doing it consistently.

Once I started making *progress* on these five goals, I was hooked on a goal-oriented lifestyle. Over the years, I added several more to this list at various points in my life. Goals gave direction to my life. I looked forward to waking up and making progress toward my goals. The process itself brought satisfaction—it was reassuring. It's like being on a train knowing where you're going. You don't worry at every station and check whether you're on the right track; you enjoy the ride.

Looking back, I realize I would not have reached where I am today without those goals. They opened the doors to a world of new opportunities.

Steve Jobs said, "We can only connect the dots looking backward." However, the flip side is also true: we can connect the dots forward through intentional goals. I experienced growth and expansion as a person through goal setting. Without them, I'd be empty. These goals were beyond my limits. They stretched me. They showed me what's possible. They helped me carve out the best version of myself and set it free by chipping away at what was in the way!

In Section 1, I share fifty-two goals I have achieved since 2003, representing a broad spectrum of my overarching life goals.

Section 2 describes a seven-step framework for goal achievement, which is my personal method for accomplishing goals. This framework has been tried and tested for over twenty years.

In Section 3, I list the top three saboteurs of goal achievement which derail goal seekers. Through coaching engagements spanning over ten years, I have observed these three challenges sabotaging people repeatedly.

After every chapter, I'll leave two questions and a quote for you to reflect upon. I highly encourage practicing the art of reflection and developing your self-knowledge.

When you complete the reflection exercise below, you'll be ready to jump into Section 1, where I'll talk about the fifty-two goals I have achieved in my life.

TIME FOR REFLECTION

- If you had a magic wand in your hand, what would you change today in your life?
- List five goals you would love to accomplish in the next three to five years.

"Without goals, and plans to reach them, you are like a ship that has set sail with no destination." - John Goddard

Section 1

Fifty-two goals

In this section, I'll share my journey of achieving fifty-two goals from 2003 to 2024. I have only listed those goals that required a significant amount of time, effort, and engagement. For brevity, I have not included many intermediate or supporting goals from this journey.

For each of these goals, I'll provide a summary of why I chose them and how I achieved them through planning, carving out time, and consistent effort.

I hope that by the time you reach the end of this section, you'll be inspired to create your list of goals. The prompts at the end of each goal will stoke your thinking. They'll help you contemplate your goals. They'll help you discover your *expansive* goals.

I'm excited to talk about my first goal! Let's go.

1

LOSING 33 POUNDS

In 2003, I started working on my first goal: to lose weight and get in shape. I felt lethargic and didn't find any interest in moving my body. It was difficult to stand straight for a few minutes. I wanted to start with something small to begin my fitness journey.

I started walking in a Bengaluru city park. The workout was not intense, however, I liked the consistency of being there every day and walking alone. No music, no talking, just listening to my own thoughts. I started with 15 minutes and increased to 45 minutes within three months. This bolstered my confidence in being consistent toward my goal. The experience of daily movement was healing. Moving in silence was meditative.

After four months, I wanted to explore other ways of exercising and see if I could trim down even further by joining a gym. I joined a gym called Super Bodies Fitness Center. Harish was the owner and trainer. He used to be a professional bodybuilder in his younger years. Harish was well-toned and super fit with biceps like large grapefruits.

I started going to the gym six days a week. My typical workout entailed 20 minutes of walking on an inclined treadmill followed by weight training for 30 minutes. This was an exciting time and I gained renewed confidence and energy to work on my goal. I lost some weight, and it felt great.

There's one strange experience worth sharing here. Whenever I was in a changing room at a clothing store, I would see myself in the mirror and wonder when I'd lose all those extra pounds of fat. A lot of it sat around my waist. It was stubborn, unwilling to budge—looking at it made me sad for a few minutes. I would console myself by saying the mirror was exaggerating and showing it out of proportion. As you can imagine, it wasn't helping. Self-pity is not the same as self-help!

This experience repeated itself every time I entered a changing room in any clothing store, creating a feeling of déjà vu. The same thoughts, feelings, and mental chatter looped through my brain and injected a heavy dose of powerlessness and hopelessness. The power of thought is incredible. It can dictate our experience and shape the way we perceive the world around us. Thoughts can linger like an icky aroma. You feel like everything about you stinks. But remember, it's all made up. The stink doesn't exist. Thoughts simply create it out of nowhere.

I lost around 18 pounds (or 8 kilograms) in nine months, which gave me hope and filled me with the energy needed to continue the journey. Until then, I thought I had no control over my weight and physique, as if it were predetermined by my genes.

Once this limiting belief was shattered, I was more open to trying new ways of exercising. I made changes to my eating habits too. The results inspired me to look for other ways to expedite my journey in weight loss. That's when I thought of signing up for a course in swimming. That's how I shredded the remaining 15 pounds (or 7 kilograms). Let's talk about that in the next chapter.

Time for reflection

- What's something you desperately wish you could change about yourself?
- How would your life change when that happens?

"We can call this 'the progress principle': Pleasure comes more from making progress toward goals than from achieving them. Shakespeare captured it perfectly: Things won are done; joy's soul lies in the doing." - Jonathan Haidt [2]

---

2   Jonathan Haidt, *The Happiness Hypothesis* (Basic Books, 2006)

2

FACING THE FEAR OF WATER

To accelerate my fitness goal and decrease my weight even further, I joined a swimming course. I had seen my cousins enjoy swimming in a lake, but I didn't have the courage to get into the water back in middle school. I was afraid of water. I was afraid I would drown while swimming. I didn't enjoy being in the water.

That's the main reason I added learning to swim to my goal list. Losing weight was a serendipitous outcome. I enrolled in a 21-day course. The classes were held at 8:30 p.m. It was an odd time to swim, but when the "why" is strong, how and when don't matter much.

There were more than 50 men in that class. It was a big swimming pool—50 feet long and 16 feet deep at the deepest end. The trainer, Ritheesh, was only nineteen, but he was a professional swimmer. His movements and speed in the water created pictures of a dolphin in my mind. Watching him swim was a joy.

The 10-minute warm-up session was interesting. I observed many other men learning to swim and felt comfortable seeing familiar body types—less fit, more fat. You see, misery loves company. Some participants gave me hope and others made me feel better about my situation.

On the third day, we were taken to the deep end. We were asked to jump and swim across 10 feet, where we would reach the other corner. I was scared. My mind filled with thoughts and pictures of me drowning. My stomach churned and my knees shivered. I started sweating.

I let other people go first and kept waiting. Finally, my turn came, I jumped reluctantly. Within five seconds of being in water, I panicked. Instead of keeping my body flat and crawling with my legs flapping in the water; I was vertical and couldn't move, I realized I was sinking. I drank some water and went down. If only I had kept my mouth closed, I could have managed to cross the 10 feet. The fear led to inaction and a downward spiral. My thoughts of drowning were close to becoming a reality.

Ritheesh jumped in the pool and dragged me to the other corner. I clutched his hand like a baby.

I was safe. It was a near-death experience for me. I thanked Ritheesh and made a silent vow to continue learning for at least a year.

I learned the basics by the end of the 21-day course and was able to swim at a six-feet depth comfortably. I still had this fear of moving to deeper ends. Logically speaking, after six feet, you can easily go to deeper pools. But the mind controls our capacity. Like an elephant controlling the rider, our minds control our actions, even though we consciously choose goals as the rider.

The drowning incident had a terrifying impact on me. Luckily, I didn't quit. I went to the pool every night for more than a year. I became proficient in freestyle, breaststroke, and backstroke swimming. I went to deeper areas of the pool gradually and finally swam at 16-feet depth. Butterfly stroke was hard to get a handle on. I stopped going to the pool after 18 months, since I had other goals to focus on. Mastering the butterfly stroke continues to be on my list.

By this time, I had lost 15 kilograms (or 33 pounds) in two years, from 2003 to 2005. I felt lighter physically and emotionally. I felt more confident about myself and what was possible in my life through the consistent action I had taken.

The key lesson: instead of *waiting to feel a certain way* before taking action, I can act as a way of creating that feeling. This key lesson was instrumental for me to continue this goal-driven journey.

TIME FOR REFLECTION

- What's your number one fear?
- How would you feel if you overcame that fear?

"Behavior wags the tail of feelings... We do, then we feel." - David K. Reynolds

A unique fact about swimming is that it is one of the few physical activities that engages almost all of the body's major muscle groups without putting stress on the joints, making it an excellent low-impact exercise suitable for people of all ages and fitness levels.

3

BECOMING A CONFIDENT
PUBLIC SPEAKER

While writing this chapter, I realized that these goals weren't sequential. Some were pursued in parallel. One goal's pursuit often affected another toward a common outcome, with that outcome itself being another goal. It was akin to a domino effect in action. One example is going to the gym and swimming to lose weight and become fit. You'll see more as you continue to read.

One of the other goals on my list was mastering public speaking. I had a glimpse of my fear during my university days when I delivered a presentation on a sorting algorithm. I wrote the algorithm on the board. I finished the entire presentation looking at the board—as if no one else was in that room. Fifty-five people were watching me, but I pretended they didn't exist, like a cat drinking milk with its eyes closed.

My fear stemmed from a technical reason: a lack of grip on the language. I learned to write and recite the English alphabet from A to Z when I was in fifth grade at the age of 11. This was common in public schools in India at that time. It's probably still true in small towns and rural areas. I was good at writing, but I had a terrible time speaking. I had a limited vocabulary, with only a few words in my arsenal for communication.

I was overly conscious about grammatical mistakes in every sentence. At times, I made more mistakes than there were words in a sentence! I'm not exaggerating in the slightest. If you're a non-native speaker, you can relate to me. English was my third language, not even my second. When I started working, this became a barrier for me. I rarely approached people to make connections. Lack of speaking skills slowly morphed into a mask of shyness, avoiding eye contact, staying away from group interactions, and not socializing with colleagues. It was the classic trap of shyness and loneliness. I labeled myself as an introvert.

During team meetings on Mondays, I struggled to give my updates to the group. Those three minutes of speaking in a group were a harrowing experience. Monday mornings were not only blue, they were also red and threatening.

My colleague at Oracle, Sumant Sarkar, asked me to attend a Toastmasters club meeting. I wasn't aware of the meeting goals and activities. I joined him on a Thursday afternoon after much prodding. I was both amazed and intimidated by some of the speakers who spoke that day. They enjoyed the limelight at the lectern, speaking fluidly for five to seven minutes. While I enjoyed listening to them, I concluded that it wasn't my cup of tea.

The impromptu speaking section was scary. The topic master could call anyone in the audience to come and speak on a random topic. I was called to speak. I wanted to run straight out of the room or vanish into thin air. Instead, I sat in my chair for a few seconds debating on my next steps. I didn't want to pass up the opportunity to face my fear. I took a few deep breaths while in my seat.

I composed myself and dragged my body to the podium. The walk from my seat to the lectern felt like running a marathon. I mumbled something for thirty seconds and rushed back to my seat. People applauded my courage to face my fear and stand there for a few seconds. I didn't like that experience, but I saw an opportunity to improve myself. The people were supportive and it was a safe place to fail, make mistakes, and become better.

The biggest benefit was listening to the grammar report at the end and learning more about the correct usage of English words and grammar. I found it was the easiest way to improve my grammar, by listening and learning from others' mistakes. Learning one new word every session through the *word of the day* was also attractive. Though I had been hesitant at the start, I was sold on the idea of Toastmasters by the end of the first session.

After a couple of sessions, I became a member in October 2003. I attended every session for the next three years and became a sponge absorbing style, structure, and language tools. I started taking meeting roles, delivered a couple of speeches, and then started leading club activities and events.

I delivered ten speeches in the first three years. Each speech was between five and seven minutes. The duration of the tenth speech was 10 minutes. To gain more practice and overcome my shyness, I attended other clubs to repeat my speeches. By the end of 2006, after three years of effort, I became a confident speaker.

This goal helped me form a new identity and showed me the way to develop new skills—consistency, incremental growth, and *learning by doing*.

I started to enjoy speaking in public. What was once fearful became a wonderful opportunity to connect with people in the audience. This goal has been the cornerstone of my confidence and self-efficacy. I was an active club member in India and the United States from 2003 to 2020. I attend club meetings occasionally as a guest now.

TIME FOR REFLECTION

- How do you feel about public speaking?
- What aspects of public speaking do you find most challenging or rewarding?

"According to most studies, people's number one fear is public speaking. Number two is death. Death is number two. Does that sound right? This means to the average person, if you go to a funeral, you're better off in the casket than doing the eulogy." - Jerry Seinfeld

The term *toastmaster* originates from the tradition of proposing toasts during formal gatherings. Initially referring to the person overseeing toasting rituals, it evolved to denote a master of ceremonies. Toastmasters International, founded by Ralph C. Smedley, continues this legacy, fostering public speaking and leadership skills worldwide through supportive clubs.

4

LEARNING A MARTIAL ART

L earning Karate was my childhood dream. I was awed by
Bruce Lee and Jackie Chan. I was looking for avenues
to channel my desire to be like them. This dream never
materialized in my childhood. We lived in a small town that
didn't have a studio for kids. As a child, I felt insecure because
I lacked the strength to defend myself if someone physically
attacked me. That's the sole reason this goal showed up on
my list. I didn't want the regret of not learning the art of
self-defense.

I started looking for a martial arts school—the style
didn't matter much to me. That's when I heard about "Krav
Maga"—an Israeli martial art. My manager at Oracle, Bence
Gazdag, was a serious practitioner and was aiming to get a
black belt in Krav.

During one of my visits to the San Francisco Bay Area,
Bence invited me to attend Krav classes at a studio in downtown
San Francisco. His friend was the trainer. I enjoyed the
60-minute intense cardio, drills, and self-defense practice
sessions. I went to two sessions and was deeply impressed by
Krav's practicality of learning and application.

I purchased a couple of books and digital videos to study
and learn more about the origin and self-defense skills taught
in Krav Maga schools. Krav Maga is unique for its practical,

simple, and aggressive self-defense techniques tailored for real-world situations.

In early 2007, a few months after my Krav classes in the US, Krav Maga classes started in Bengaluru. It was a 90-minute drive to the studio—three hours round trip. The desire was so high, the distance didn't matter. I went to the studio and immediately signed up for a six-month program. I attended weekend classes on Saturday and Sunday—six hours every weekend.

Learning Krav Maga was an exhilarating experience. It injected a strong dose of self-efficacy and a sense of confidence I never felt in my life prior to this point. I cleared three tests in two years and earned three belts with pride.

I trained with female students, a soldier from the Indian Army special forces, and even had close interactions with celebrity teachers from India and Israel. These were unique adventures in my life—until then my life was filled with academic focus and getting a well-paying job. There was a stark difference in my interest and engagement.

During one training session, the head trainer kicked my groin for a demonstration. Despite wearing a guard, the pain was unbearable, and it took me nearly fifteen minutes to recover enough to be able to walk again. That's the intensity of Krav—there are no rules, anything is allowed when it comes to saving yourself. In a sparring session, I accidentally punched someone in the nose, causing it to bleed. We were practicing at a slow pace, but I went a bit overboard during that session.

The training was all about assessing danger, training under pressure so you are prepared for a real fight, and getting into a fight when there's no other option to save yourself. Awareness of my surroundings and knowing exits in public places became second nature.

Even today, I assess a hotel room right after we arrive. Threat awareness and assessment became a new habit. This applies to many other scenarios. Your presence of mind sharpens when you apply Krav skills to life situations. You're not scared. You're more aware of the world around you.

I trained for three years to pursue this goal and fulfilled my childhood dream of learning a martial art. I learned the art of self-defense and felt a renewed level of self-confidence in the process. I wasn't insecure anymore. I had the strength and skills to save myself if needed. I felt victorious!

06/11/2009

TIME FOR REFLECTION

- Which childhood dreams have you buried alive?
- What if you attempted to make progress on one of those dreams this year?

"Krav Maga heightens perception and transforms fear into something more productive." - Imi Lichtenfeld

Krav Maga is Hebrew: *Krav* means "combat," *Maga* means "contact." It translates to "contact combat," a practical self-defense system.

5

DONATING BLOOD 50
TIMES BEFORE TURNING 50

When I was a teenager, my paternal uncle, Sriram underwent surgery. It was a struggle to find blood donors during that time. I remember my father running around the city, knocking on the doors of blood banks, and exploring any option he could think of. When a person agreed to donate, he was a hero. He saved my uncle's life!

Uncle Sriram went under the knife one more time after two years, I had just turned 18 and was eligible to donate blood. That 20 minutes of blood donation gave me a sense of pride. I was thrilled for the opportunity to help my uncle. I realized that donating blood was like lighting a candle. A candle doesn't lose anything by lighting more candles. It helps other candles glow and makes the world brighter.

Before setting this goal, I had donated six times in three years from 1998 to 2001. Since I had no goal, I wasn't consistent. I didn't donate between 2001 and 2003—not even once. What a mistake!

I set a goal of donating 50 units of blood before I turn 50. As I wrote this goal, the movie of my second donation in the year 1998 played in my mind. The satisfaction of adding years to someone's life that I experienced during the second donation inspired me to write this goal. I'll narrate the experience below.

When I was in university as an undergraduate student, I became friends with a social service volunteer. He was the coordinator for incoming requests for blood donors. There was a need for a unit of A positive blood, so I went in to help. I donated the blood directly to the lab.

During the process, the staff shared a few details about the patient—a young girl, only five years old, who had recently gone through heart surgery. Both parents were construction workers, earning daily wages through their hard work. They had great difficulty arranging three units of blood, mine was number three. They also had to spend money getting the previous two units—I felt their pain. That was the moment I decided to donate blood regularly as long as I could.

I came out of the room and sat in the rest area. A couple came to meet me, and I knew they were the parents of the little girl who would get a portion of my blood. Words cannot describe the air in the room and feelings in my heart. With folded hands, they expressed their gratitude and thanked me for saving their daughter. For them, it was surprising to see a 19-year-old doing this for a stranger as a compassionate service. I could see tears of gratitude and hope in the mother's eyes.

They had brought a couple of tender coconuts and some bananas with them as a token of gratitude. I asked them to keep the food for themselves and the little girl since they needed them more than I did.

They insisted I take them, saying, "God will punish us, he sent you to save us. Allow us to offer what we have." I still remember the eyes of that woman. I accepted the coconut water. I wasn't hungry so I didn't take the bananas they offered.

The mother carefully filled a glass with coconut water and offered it to me. I sat there in the room looking at this couple while sipping the coconut water. It was the sweetest coconut water I have ever tasted in my life.

When I wrote this goal, there was no logic behind it. Fifty was a number pulled out of thin air. I found the number reasonable and I was at number six at the time. The goal was written to ensure I made progress and continued this act of service.

By writing this goal in 2003, I became consistent with my donations every year. It inspired me to stay healthy, maintain my fitness, and make progress on the goal. I added years to others' lives through my blood and that activity added life to my years. Every time I donate blood, I sense the presence of that couple. They remind me that it matters to patients and their loving parents.

As of 2024, I have donated 50 times at age 44. With a goal, the number increased from 6 to 50, in 21 years.

That means I could now aim for 75 before 50. Or maybe 100 before 50! That's how goals are. When you focus on achieving your goals, they expand, and in the process, you also expand and surpass your limits.

TIME FOR REFLECTION

- In what ways are you interested in contributing to the community?
- If you haven't donated blood yet, would you consider trying it at least once?

"The feeling of donating blood is like no other feeling. It's like saving a life, and you don't have to be a superhero to do that." - Unknown

A unique fact about blood donation is that just one donation can save up to three lives. When you donate blood, it can be separated into its components: red blood cells, plasma, and platelets. These components can be used individually for patients with different needs, maximizing the impact of a single donation. This makes blood donation a powerful act of giving that can have a far-reaching effect on the health and well-being of multiple patients.

6

LEARNING SANSKRIT

Learning a new language was one of my goals. I already knew Kannada, Hindi, and English and was looking for one more to add. I started researching Spanish and French. They seemed fancy to learn. There was a language school in Bengaluru teaching international languages.

One day while chanting Sanskrit slokas (or verses in English), I had a realization. I had been chanting slokas since second grade, maybe earlier. I was born in a household where chanting was common and it was celebrated. My father taught me and my brother several slokas during our summer holidays during middle school. But I didn't know the meaning of what I recited—the sounds, the rhythm, and the meter kept me going.

Now, I was ready to learn the meaning and add more mojo to the experience of chanting. So I decided to learn the Sanskrit language. It was like discovering a diamond in my own backyard, something I had totally ignored. Learning Sanskrit opened a portal for exploring ancient scriptures in the Hindu religion.

To my surprise, there was a school in Bengaluru, Samskrita Bharati, dedicated to teaching Sanskrit through conversations. I joined a 90-day course. It was six hours a week of live classes spread over Saturday and Sunday. The first class was a unique experience. For 3 hours, the instructor spoke simple Sanskrit sentences to teach and have conversations with students. I could understand most of it, since many words in Kannada and Hindi are derived from Sanskrit. It was teaching by immersion, education through conversation. I loved this method! It inspired me to continue.

Overjoyed by the first class, I started speaking simple sentences in Sanskrit. It was a surreal feeling to speak Sanskrit. I slowed down while chanting to break the words up, so I could understand various words. Subsequently, I tried to separate nouns, verbs, and adjectives in a verse. It was a fun exercise. I thoroughly enjoyed the process of learning. I discovered the joy of learning something other than computer programming languages like C, C++, Java, and others.

There were several activities during the 90-day course to immerse us in the language, including a short play with Sanskrit dialogues. The instructor and a few students encouraged me to learn further since I seemed to show intense interest and natural talent. This was an example of how others' perceptions can help you in a favorable way. I was inspired to learn more, put in more effort, and develop my Sanskrit vocabulary. The more I invested, the better I became.

I continued learning Sanskrit for three years. I still remember the teacher proudly giving me the certificate after Level 1 saying, "You have done great, your fundamentals are strong. Keep going." And I did. I achieved three levels in the Samskrita Bharati curriculum. The highlight of the journey was me getting the highest score in their written test—twice!

I had challenged myself to learn a new language, and I really enjoyed it! I loved chanting even more because I was able to understand and articulate what I was reciting. In addition to the sound, the meaning and feeling brought fresh energy when I chanted slokas. I would not have experienced this joy, had I not set a goal of learning a new language, which led me to this wonderful experience.

With this goal, I was able to read Sanskrit literature and then leverage this skill to achieve the next two goals. This goal also revealed to me the possibility of teaching Sanskrit to beginners in my fifties and sixties. I know I would love the experience of teaching!

TIME FOR REFLECTION

- Have you ever dreamt of achieving fluency in another language? If so, which language, and why?
- How can you make progress toward this goal?

"Sanskrit is the greatest language of the world." - Max Muller

The word *Sanskrit* comes from the Sanskrit language itself. In Sanskrit, the term is written as *sa⊠sk⊠ta* (**संस्कृत**), which means "refined, cultivated, or perfected." The word is derived from the root *samskr* (**संस्कृ**), which means "to make perfect, to polish, or to refine."

7

READING *THE BHAGAVAD GITA*

When I learned about John Goddard's life list, I was impressed with his well-rounded exploration of life. John studied spirituality. He studied scriptures and dug deep into his own faith. When I wrote my life list, I added learning Sanskrit for the same reason. It was a goal to achieve larger goals. An instrument for spiritual exploration. A way to understand the wisdom in Sanskrit literature.

I had heard about *The Bhagavad Gita*. The *Bhagavad Gita* is the most famous of all Indian scriptures and is universally regarded as one of the world's spiritual and literary masterpieces. It has been translated into more than seventy-five languages. It has 18 chapters that contain 700 verses.

The *Gita* opens on the eve of a mighty battle when the warrior Arjuna is overwhelmed by despair and refuses to fight. He turns to his charioteer, Krishna, who counsels him on why he must fight. In the dialogue that follows, Arjuna comes to realize that the true battle is for his own soul.

Previously, I had recited some well-known verses without knowing what they meant. Chanting felt good and I kept doing it. That's the beauty of sounds in Sanskrit. The language has healing sounds and the healing power multiplies once you know the meaning of the words. Meaning adds potency to the benefits of chanting. It certainly did for me.

The desire to understand the meaning of verses from the *Gita* kept me going in the quest of learning Sanskrit. Many times, I felt like stopping. It was difficult to remember the meanings of words and continue learning. Dedicating eight to ten hours a week to this purpose was not easy.

But I was hopeful; I knew it was a matter of time. More importantly, I was confident the attempt was totally worth it. I knew that one day I would be able to read the *Gita* and understand it without translation or with minimal reliance on translation. I started reading the *Gita*, on my own, after a year of learning Sanskrit. I was thrilled to be able to do that. Sanskrit became my fourth language.

I have read the *Gita* cover-to-cover several hundred times over the years. Sometimes for wisdom, sometimes for lifting the mood through healing sounds, and sometimes for reminding me of the power of spirit.

Even now, I pick up the book and start with any chapter I'm called to read. When fear, doubt or insecurity strikes my mind, I read a chapter of *Gita*. To me, it's a verbal meditation. Chanting verses from the *Gita* is healing and therapeutic.

Gita has verses covering various aspects of life. One of my favorite verses is below (Devanagari script, transliteration followed by its translation in English).

कर्मण्येवाधिकारस्ते मा फलेषु कदाचन ।
मा कर्मफलहेतुर्भूर्मा ते संगोऽस्त्वकर्मणि ॥

karmaṇyevādhikāraste mā phaleṣu kadācana |
mā karmaphalaheturbhūrmā te saṅgo'stvakarmaṇi ||

You have the right only to your action, but never to its fruits. Do not let the fruits of action be your motive, nor become attached to inaction.

This verse is a great reminder to focus on action. Do what's in our control and stay away from the lure of inaction.

One other gem from *Gita* (Devanagari script, transliteration followed by its translation in English).

युक्ताहारविहारस्य युक्तचेष्टस्य कर्मसु।
युक्तस्वप्नावबोधस्य योगो भवति दु:खहा॥

yuktāhāravihārasya yuktace⊠asya karmasu |
yuktasvapnāvabodhasya yogo bhavati du:khahā ||

He who is regulated in his habits of eating, sleeping, recreation, and work can mitigate all material pains by practicing the yoga system.

There are many quotable quotes in *Gita*. It's filled with wisdom.

I'm so glad to have added this goal to my list. My life has improved. I found wisdom, serenity, and connection to the spirit.

TIME FOR REFLECTION

- What spiritual scriptures or literature inspires you?
- Is there a spiritual goal that appeals to you?

"In the morning, I bathe my intellect in the stupendous and cosmogonal philosophy of the Bhagavad-gita, in comparison with which our modern world and its literature seem puny and trivial." - Henry David Thoreau

Bhagavad Gita derives from Sanskrit: *Bhagavad* means "divine or fortunate," and *Gita* means "song or recital." Thus, it translates to "The Divine Song" or "The Song of the Lord."

8

READING *THE KAMA SUTRA*

H
ave you read *The Kama Sutra?* The answer is most likely no, but I'm sure you have at least heard about it. The word is popular all over the world. *The Kama Sutra* is an ancient Indian text on sexuality and emotional fulfillment in life.

Attributed to Vatsyayana, *The Kama Sutra* was written as a guide to the art of living well, the nature of love, finding a life partner, and maintaining one's love life. I wish this were taught in college. Luckily, I covered this subject on my own.

I was surprised to see a bar named Kama Sutra in the Netherlands while I was visiting in 2006. The word evokes a sense of wonder, awe, and sensuality. It paints pictures in our minds. Most of those pictures are influenced by what we see and hear from other people on this through movies, books, and social media.

If you are keen to know what's special about Kama Sutra, pick up a book and read. That's exactly what I did after two years of learning Sanskrit. All over the world, people talk about this book; very few have read it. The day I saw the bar in the Netherlands, I was inspired to read the book. Reading it felt like a great adventure and hence it became a goal.

I asked around the Sanskrit community and found a book that had original verses in Sanskrit along with Hindi translation and word-by-word explanation in Hindi. This helped me avoid seeing the source through the lens of a translator. I could read it myself in Sanskrit and occasionally lean on the Hindi translation to confirm my understanding.

Vatsyayana's work is phenomenal. The book is full of short verses. It's really gripping. Once you start, it's difficult to put the book down. Several cultural codes in married couples and wedding rituals in India are neatly described in this book.

The goal of this chapter is not to encapsulate the book's summary, so I won't attempt that. I strongly recommend reading this book. You don't have to be picky like me. Pick up any author's work on this subject. Preferably choose the one that translates the original verses as opposed to commentary. Regardless of your age, gender, and interests, this masterpiece has something to offer to you.

Toward the end, Vatsyayana says this in a verse (Devanagari script, transliteration followed by its translation in English).

परस्परानुकूल्येन तथा तुल्यापमानयो: |
सम्वत्सरशतेनापि प्रीतिर्न परिहीयते ||

parasparānukūlyena tathā tulyapamānayo⊠ |
samvatsarashatenāpi prītirna parihīyate ||

Mutual cooperation and equality in giving and receiving, even for a hundred years, love does not diminish.

This is pure gold. One wouldn't expect such sage advice in a book that's written on sexuality and emotional fulfillment in life.

A relationship has two legs: love and respect. You can walk together for a hundred years and beyond. This advice has certainly shaped my relationship with Anusha. We have learned a lot from each other. We have supported each other to be the best version of ourselves, and the journey continues.

TIME FOR REFLECTION

- Are there any books you want to read? What is stopping you?
- Which ones can you read this year?

"'The Kama Sutra' reveals the profound and timeless wisdom of ancient India on love, relationships, and human nature." - Deepak Chopra

Kama Sutra stems from Sanskrit: *Kama* for "desire or pleasure" and *Sutra* for "thread or manual." Hence, it means "The Treatise on Desire" or "The Manual of Pleasure," concerning sexuality and relationships.

9

Playing a musical instrument

My father played the harmonium; he was really good. I saw his stage performances a few times in my childhood. We had a harmonium at home. I wanted to learn how to play it. I started with the basics in sixth grade, but for some reason, I didn't pursue it with passion. I learned the keyboard for a few months in high school but didn't learn enough to play songs on it. Playing songs on the keyboard remained a distant dream.

I wanted to make it a reality through a goal. Learning to play a musical instrument found a place on my list. I chose the keyboard for this goal since I liked it better than the harmonium. My goal was to play 50 songs on the keyboard. Fifty was good enough to keep me motivated to stay on the path for two years. My focus was more on the process, less on the outcome.

I joined a music school. I had one class every Wednesday evening. This was a unique experience. I was the *only* adult student in the class—all the remaining students were under fifteen. It required a different kind of energy and humility to be in the studio learning with the kids. Some kids were way ahead of me. The teachers interacted with each student on their skill level. Increasing my skill level became important to me. I wanted to get more attention from the teacher.

The teacher understood my goal—to be capable of playing *fifty* songs on the keyboard. Whatever exercises the teacher gave me, I promptly practiced in the class and at home every day. In a few months, I had improved my finger movement and played the tunes in various scales. I was ready for the next level—playing songs.

It was a dream come true! The teacher had a list of English, Hindi, and Kannada songs. I didn't have the liberty to bring my own favorites. I had to pick from what was available. My first song was "My Heart Will Go On" from the movie *The Titanic*. It was a beautiful song. I played it over and over to ensure I got the song right and played it smoothly. Every time I played that song, the feeling of living my dream washed over me. I felt I could do anything with a goal.

I kept learning a few more songs. I really enjoyed my time in the studio and practicing at home. Over time, I had close to 50 songs on my list to play. I did it well, enjoyed the experience, and it showed when I was on the keyboard.

I also did one public performance in front of 200 people for a corporate event at Oracle. I performed three songs on my keyboard in 15 minutes. I never imagined playing an instrument in front of 200 people. It just happened out of nowhere. I was well prepared and the opportunity knocked on the door. I grabbed the opportunity without hesitation. It was a moment to cherish—the audience's applause, encouragement, and appreciation were exhilarating. I felt like a *rockstar* on the stage. I wish my father could see me perform at this event; he would be beaming with pride and satisfaction.

I scratched off one more goal from my list in *style*. I had developed a new skill—a skill I never would have gained without it appearing on my list. It happened only because

I added it to my goals list and took decisive and consistent action for two years.

TIME FOR REFLECTION

- Which musical instrument did you dream of playing in your childhood?
- What if you add this as a goal? What if you learned to play one song on your favorite musical instrument? How would you feel?

"Music expresses that which cannot be said and on which it is impossible to be silent." - Victor Hugo

10

BECOMING A HUMOROUS SPEAKER

I n the world of Toastmasters, *a humorous speaker* is someone who can entertain the audience and make them laugh. It involves telling them clean jokes and incorporating self-deprecating humor. It's like being a stand-up comedian during a speech.

Goal setting has a domino effect. One goal could nudge us to consider other related goals. For example, when I reached the initial goal in public speaking, achieving the Competent Communicator certification with ten speeches, I saw a common thread in my speeches. They were all about either motivation or information. I wanted to expand my range of topics and skills in speaking. I didn't want to be boxed in the category of "motivational speaker." I felt it was limiting. I saw accomplished speakers in Toastmasters clubs who added a hint of humor to land a better impact on the audience.

I chose humorous speaking as a track for my advanced speech projects. This was clearly not up my alley. It was like asking a fish to climb a tree—or so I thought. Still, I pursued it. My friend and colleague Swaroop Malangi recommended reading P.G. Wodehouse's books to flex my humor muscles. Swaroop had an uncanny skill of adding humor through his words. So, his recommendation carried weight. I started reading Wodehouse's books. I loved his humor and I was blown away by his ability to paint pictures via words and inject humor through figurative writing.

Wodehouse peppered his writing with figurative language (vivid descriptions, similes, and metaphors). You would see one in every three to five lines, painting vivid pictures as you read. And you'll remember them, even after several weeks. His writing gets tattooed in your consciousness. It certainly did on mine. I hope you're noticing his influence while you're engrossed in this book.

I still remember a sentence from his book, "He had the look of one who had drunk the cup of life and found a dead beetle at the bottom." [3] I gathered many tools from his writing. I applied them to my speeches and rehearsed my timing, proper delivery of punchlines, and purposeful pauses.

The result was evident. The club members loved my clean, simple, and self-deprecating humor. I enjoyed the process of finding topics, collecting material, and stringing a speech to evoke laughter.

My wife Anusha has been a pillar of support for my goals. She ordered a dozen books authored by P.G. I devoured them. I remember a couple of speeches where she enjoyed being among the audience.

I was no longer caged as a motivational speaker. I had a new identity: an *entertaining speaker*. It's crazy how we put labels on ourselves and define our *personalities*, as if we are etched in stone and fixed forever.

I scripted one speech about marriage for a humorous speech contest. It was a big hit. *People loved it.* I won the first prize at club and area-level speaking contests.

---

3   P.G. Wodehouse, *The Man Upstairs and Other Stories* (Bibliotech Press)

The division level was something new to me—speaking to 300 people from a large stage with a collar mic. To say "I prepared well" would be an understatement. We were newly married in 2008 and I wanted Anusha to witness my best performance on stage. I put in a ton of effort.

I visited the auditorium a day before the event to assess the environment. I went up on stage and stood there for over 10 minutes; this is a common technique used by seasoned speakers. The effort paid off. I had no fear or worries during my speech. I felt as if it were my second attempt at the speech, since I had been on the stage the day before. That's the power of being fully prepared. Anusha enjoyed my speech. I loved every moment of my speech performance. I got the second runner-up award that day.

It was a testimony to the power of goal-setting and consistent effort. I considered myself a serious person, only talking about important topics that mattered in life. Others had similar views. Now, it was not just the audience that thought I was a humorous speaker, I believed it too. It was the result of a goal, effort, support, and stretching beyond my comfort zone. I went beyond my own perceived limits!

TIME FOR REFLECTION

- How do you see your personality: fixed or changeable?
- What would change in your life if you started being a bit more humorous or light-hearted?

"Humor is the salt of life, and without it, everything becomes flat, dull, and tasteless." - P.G. Wodehouse

11

DOING A COURSE IN BUSINESS WEAR

I moved to a different team at Oracle in 2006. This role required a broad knowledge of several business systems: marketing, sales, finance, and customer support. The new role involved international travel two or three times a year. In that role, I used to interact with senior leaders from several business units. I didn't want to walk around like a college kid wearing jeans and a graphic t-shirt. Socializing for lunch or dinner was a way to build relationships and rapport not just in the company, but outside it as well.

Our conferences were held in five-star hotels and I wanted to understand more about two specific things. I'll cover one here and the second one will be covered in the next chapter. First, I wanted to improve my business-dressing skills. That was an important skill for me to learn at that point. I was at level zero in this area.

Once I set the goal, I started finding people who could offer guidance in this area. I learned about Sudhir Udayakanth in the city, who conducted a one-day workshop on dressing for business. The highlight of the course was a four-hour trip with him to a men's clothing store which helped me understand the nuances of style and fashion. I was clueless about those aspects.

Having someone to guide me through it was exciting. I wore sneakers and chinos most of the time. They were fully uncoordinated and it was clearly evident. I had seen this during my first trip to Singapore in the new role. I was the odd man out among well-dressed professionals from various countries at the first conference. I didn't want to repeat that on my next trip. I needed to change. I was *ready* to change.

During the first half, Sudhir shared excellent information about formal, semi-formal, and casual wear. I listened to him with a gaping mouth. I mixed all three styles in my dressing. That was my signature style. The attire looked mixed up and I looked messed up.

He then went over accessories, choosing colors from top to bottom and making sure they matched. I felt like a kid who just learned a bunch of new tricks to solve a Rubik's cube. I asked questions and made detailed notes. You might think I'm exaggerating, but for six years I had such an intense focus on academics that there was nothing else on my mind. All these ideas during the workshop were exciting to learn and implement. They were practical and useful in life.

After lunch, we went to a clothing store where I learned about the clear differences and reasons for jeans, formal trousers, chinos, and other casual wear. Feeling the clothing running under my fingertips, understanding the stitching patterns, and listening to Sudhir's explanation was a wonderful integration of theory and the validation of that theory in real products in the store.

It was a day filled with learning, experimenting, and achieving another goal. The goal of understanding business attire and being aware of my choices in the future was complete.

This one-day workshop increased my self-confidence. I didn't make radical changes after the course. I experimented with tiny changes in the next few months, and the results were visible in my clothing choices. It reflected in the way I saw myself, shaping my self-image and self-perception.

The change after this training: I walked with my head held high at the next business conference. I was no longer the odd man in conferences. I felt like a business professional because I started *behaving* like one. I no longer felt like a college student who had sneaked into a business event to enjoy the free food. Speaking of food, let's go to the next chapter.

TIME FOR REFLECTION

- What skills do you want to improve, and what's stopping you?
- When you master this skill, how would your life change?

"You can never be overdressed or overeducated." - Oscar Wilde

12

DOING A COURSE IN DINING ETIQUETTE

The second workshop from Sudhir was on dining etiquette. I felt the need for this one, too, as I attended international conferences and met colleagues for dinner and lunch. At a young age, I had the opportunity to network with executives at Oracle. I didn't want to harm this opportunity with my unpolished etiquette. I was representing India in these conferences. I wanted to become a citizen of the world—a cosmopolitan. For some of you this may be common knowledge, for me it was Greek and Latin.

The workshop began with the basics of fine dining and table manners. I still remember the PowerPoint slide with a dinner plate and all the surrounding silverware. I learned the logic behind various sizes of plates, bowls, spoons, knives, and forks. That's the day I realized forks and spoons have different purposes. I never used a fork. The art of drinking soup, filling my spoon from the bowl with an inside-out movement, was a revelation for me.

Using forks from left to right, using the napkin appropriately, and providing signals from the way I left my fork and knife on the plate. I had mixed feelings—excitement over learning new things and overwhelm about not being able to remember everything. Fortunately, the excitement got the better of me and I enjoyed the session.

We covered so much in that workshop. The dos and don'ts of eating were educational, especially tips around hygiene, keeping hands on the table, and not making noise while eating. Hilarious discussion in the room brought memories of me and others indulging in such behaviors without awareness.

There was so much to learn in this domain. I had an open mind to embrace these ideas and understand the rationale behind these etiquettes. Otherwise, it's easy to dismiss them as a vanity affair and argue for eating with fingers. It's an open mind that helps us grow. Listen, learn, integrate, and leverage what works. That's my way of thinking. The more open we are, the wider the perspective we develop over time. We don't want to be a frog in the well; do we?

We had lunch together at a fine-dining restaurant. That's when I could implement all the ideas from the workshop into practice. It was a meal to remember and celebrate—another goal achieved from my list.

I still follow many of the things I learned on that day. They became habits over the years. One good thing about writing this story, when my son Samyak reads this, he'll know why I ask him to follow a few specific rules at the dinner table, regardless of where we are eating. Some etiquettes are good to follow everywhere, after all.

You can guess what happened in my future international conferences. I enjoyed dinner conversations. I was less focused on *myself* and more focused on learning about other people.

As a natural outcome, I nurtured great relationships with other departmental leaders. I stopped resisting social hours. They were great opportunities for nourishing relationships with colleagues.

Time for reflection

- Which course or training have you thought about taking, and why?
- What if you make that your goal for this year?

"Good manners are just a way of showing other people that we have respect for them." - Bill Kelly

13

BECOMING A WORKSHOP FACILITATOR

While I was active in Toastmasters club activities, I realized I could help new members with speech writing and delivery skills. I conducted a few educational sessions on preparing speeches and delivering them. I also created a short training on impromptu speaking.

These were simple ideas, yet super practical since I had used them for three to four years. The result was evident in the joy I exuded on the stage. People enjoyed the sessions and I saw their transformation within a few weeks. Several club members leapfrogged and showed great improvement in their speech content and delivery. I was moonlighting as a trainer and workshop facilitator, although unpaid. It was a perfect outlet for self-expression. I enjoyed helping others. Self awareness is key, you need to notice what brings you joy. *Joy is your compass.*

In the year 2008, a few months after Anusha and I got married, I wanted to experiment with earning income as a leadership and communications trainer. It was on my list. It was an experiment to see if I could earn money through helping others in effective communication and time management.

Since I had a few workshops under my belt, I approached the training companies in the city to partner with them. Surprisingly, not many were willing to consider external trainers who had their own content. I was unfazed by rejection. I kept knocking on several doors to search for one that could open a new opportunity for me. My goal was to be a consulting trainer.

During a lunch meeting with Sudhir (whom I mentioned in the previous two chapters), I expressed my interest in training and shared my workshop details. Sudhir immediately offered an option to conduct a session on *Time Management*. I already had a workshop based on my experience in time management, self-discipline, and goal achievement.

My workshop was launched and we were expecting 10 people in the first workshop. Only *one* registered. Sudhir asked me, "Do you want to teach one person or move this to another date?"

I insisted on doing it for one person. Imagine me teaching one person in a small conference room. Sudhir watched me run the show for four hours, enjoying my time and engaging the *only* student in the room. I was driven by passion and joy. The number of people didn't matter at all. I was serving one person with my expertise and that's all that mattered to me.

Over lunch, Sudhir appreciated my passion, teaching style, and personal examples during the four-hour workshop. He validated my passion for teaching through example. After lunch, he wrote a check for 800 Indian Rupees (the equivalent of 15 US dollars back then). I grasped the check in my hand and experienced goosebumps coursing through my body. I had proven that I could earn money through training others! Without a written goal, I wouldn't even think about this goal, let alone persistently pursue it.

Most trainers are attached to their slides, they don't share with anyone. I openly shared mine with Sudhir saying,

"For my audience, I am the message. My slides are a way to connect with them." Sudhir was surprised to see my self-confidence and self-belief. He said I was the first trainer he had seen in a decade who was willing to share his materials. I am inspired by Dr. Marshall Goldsmith and his work, and I follow his practices. Like him, I give away all my training materials to anyone who asks.

With this milestone, I was a consulting trainer. I did a few assignments with other training companies in the same year. More doors opened through referrals and connections.

Despite being busy with a full-time job, I managed to explore alternative avenues to leverage my career capital and strengths. This was possible because of my clear sense of direction. I was ready to conduct experiments and collect data by setting specific goals. I took *full ownership* of my career path.

TIME FOR REFLECTION

- What is your number one skill, and do people often seek your advice in specific areas? Is this because you are considered an expert in those areas?
- How can you get paid for what you love doing?

"Facilitation is not about having all the answers; it's about asking the right questions and fostering meaningful dialogue."
- Unknown

14

LEARNING FROM A MISSED GOAL

S o far, I have only talked about goals I was able to achieve through consistent effort and incremental improvement. I feel compelled to share an example where I didn't achieve a goal and had a clear reason not to pursue it after only one attempt. It is an example of *strategic quitting*. I'll share more about strategic quitting in Section 2 as part of the seven-step framework for goal achievement. This story will show that it's not just about achieving the goal, it's what we become during the process that is exciting.

I wanted to win the 2009 World Championship in public speaking. This is a worldwide contest organized by Toastmasters International organization. Thousands of people around the world compete in this contest, starting at their local club level until only ten finalists are selected for the final round to compete for the world champion trophy. To me, this was a worthy goal to pursue considering my struggle with effective communication. It was an opportunity to show people what's possible, especially all the people who struggle with English as their second or third language. I wanted to be a beacon of hope.

At the time, people picked inspirational speeches with personal stories to engage the audience, making an impact and a strong call to action at the end.

I wrote a 650-word speech to ensure I finished in under seven minutes. It was my hero's journey overcoming the fear of public speaking and how this journey led to new opportunities and life experiences. I had a couple of other anecdotes, including Hellen Keller's story. The speech was titled *Kill the Beast*. I won the club-level contest and moved on to the area level.

The quality of speech script and performance elevate as we go up to subsequent levels in this contest. I modified a few things and won the first prize at the area level too. That's when I hired a coach, Ian Faria, to help me get to the division level. Once I crossed the division level, I would need to win at three more levels to speak in the world champion contest.

At the time, Ian Faria was a popular coach and corporate trainer in India. He had also won several contests, including a world championship in a taped speech category. Ian was super helpful in shaping my script and style of delivery. He also recommended neutralizing my accent to ensure it didn't shred my chances of winning at higher levels. When words aren't clearly enunciated, they diminish the impact and lose points from contest judges.

I worked with an accent coach for a few weeks. Because I had studied English at age 11 and didn't have a solid foundation in the language, I had picked up a lot of mispronunciations. We started correcting one at a time. The accent coach wanted me to pick an American accent. For me, this was a hard nut to crack. Reluctantly, I tried for a few days. It was unnatural and far away from my natural way of speaking and narrating my story. It was like putting lipstick on a pig; too artificial.

After a few sessions, I realized I was being too conscious of my accent and enunciation. I was doing it at the expense of joy, connection, and a wonderful opportunity to share my story with the audience. That was too costly, so I asked the coach to limit the scope to accent neutralization. We steered away from putting on an American accent. That helped me return to the original goal of sharing a story of action and inspiration. In other words, I minimized my weakness by neutralizing the accent and focused on magnifying my strengths.

I didn't get the first prize in the division-level contest. The effort I put into preparing certainly helped. With several changes in my enunciation, I could now communicate to an international audience with confidence. It was the most significant advantage of pursuing this goal. Like I said in the beginning of this chapter, it's what we *become* during the process that is exciting and equally valuable.

The whole idea of 10 people judging speeches and scoring on seven parameters was very subjective in these contests. The effort behind contests wasn't something I wanted to repeat. This awareness helped me stop pursuing this goal. It was a strategic choice to quit the game.

So, I moved on to other goals and never pursued this goal again. I'm sharing this for context. Some goals are not worth pursuing. No one else can decide for you. You have to make that call. You're the creator in charge. You're the artist of your life, painting the canvas of life with your cherished goals, one stroke at a time!

Time for reflection

- Are you pursuing goals that may not be worth the effort? Is this pursuit for your own satisfaction or to meet someone else's expectations?
- How would your life change if you forgave yourself and ceased the pursuit of those goals?

"It turns out that the process of working toward a goal, participating in a valued and challenging activity, is as important to well-being as its attainment." - Sonja Lyubomirsky

15

SAYING *NO* TO TV

Once I was hooked on personal goals in 2004 (a year after writing the first five goals), I lost interest in watching movies and television shows. In the movie of life, with a list of goals, I was *the hero*. I didn't want heroic stimulation through movies and shows. I also didn't like any of the televised entertainment because my life was filled with entertainment. Does that sound extreme? Not really. When you pursue a goal with passion, your life turns around. You want to wake up knowing your day has interesting challenges in the pursuit of your cherished dreams. Each goal adds a brick to your life wall. If you build the brick right, the wall will take care of itself.

Not watching TV was easy as a bachelor since I had a strong conviction about it. I was really worried about turning my back on this decision post-wedding. Anusha was (to some extent still is) a big Bollywood movie buff. She was shocked to hear I didn't own a TV and didn't like spending time in front of it.

When we got married in 2008, I asked her if we could attempt living without a TV at home, just for a few months to see what it feels like. We were both software engineers—busy jobs, busy minds, and looming deadlines. To my delight, she agreed. And our life *flourished*.

Looking back, I feel she agreed out of love and respect for me. That was a strange thing for her. We still laugh at it now, but she also agrees that we have gained a lot from that decision.

Every evening, I was done with work by 6:00 p.m., even when I worked from home. I would pick Anusha up from the shuttle drop-off point and we would do something fun and exciting every evening—eating out, visiting friends or family, going to temples, walking in parks, playing card games, and watching live theater performances.

We never ran out of ideas. We found things to keep us engaged and engrossed, being together and learning about each other. Celebrating *our life* vs celebrating *others' lives* on TV. It was incredible! Anusha didn't love it as much in the beginning, but later she liked it, too. So, we continued. The tradition continued even when we moved to the United States.

Samyak was born in a house without a TV. We found alternatives for his edutainment. He uses a laptop for watching shows or videos on weekends. We join him to watch his choice of movies (or Anusha's choice of Bollywood comedy movies) or shows on a large display. It's a large screen, not a TV with a cable connection.

Not owning a TV (and not subscribing to a cable connection) is one of the best decisions in our family life. We have so much time together. We cook, play card games, eat, go for walks, read books, and do what fills our heart.

Our family's favorite pastime is to sit in a coffee shop to play card games, drink hot chocolate, and then read a book of our choice.

When Samyak was in first grade, I read books to him every night. We finished reading eight books by Roald Dahl that year. We went to bed at seven each night. I read a book aloud for ninety minutes in bed, then we read many nonfiction fables together—for several months! It was the best time of our lives—laughing and learning through reading. This time wouldn't have been available if we had the habit of watching TV every evening. We would have lost so much time by watching others have fun on a screen (doing what they love doing—acting).

Here's my view: My family and I want to *choose* when and what to watch. I don't want the TV to *choose* us. I want us to have the privilege of choice and exercise that privilege. We carve out time on weekends for entertainment and enjoy our time together as a family watching movies and shows.

Until his second grade, Samyak thought only privileged people owned a TV. We had to explain to him several times about our conscious choice, the rationale, and its impact. I hope one day he appreciates the decision and replicates it.

I hope my example inspires you to start your hero's journey by being strategic about spending time on entertainment and investing time in what truly matters to you. You don't need to throw away your TV; you just need to prioritize what matters to you. We are the heroes we look for in movies!

TIME FOR REFLECTION

- How many hours do you watch TV (or other entertainment) every week?
- What if you invested this time in your goals? What if you started with just 20 percent daily?

"I find television very educational. Every time somebody turns on the set, I go into the other room and read a book." - Groucho Marx

16

Visiting Sri Lanka

International travel was one of my goals; especially traveling in style with Anusha. The first place on my list was Sri Lanka, although Anusha keeps reminding me her go-to place would have been Maldives. I had heard a lot about Sri Lanka's beauty and that's why it was on the top of my list. One important aspect of our trip was luxury. I wanted to ensure we got a royal experience during the trip. This means we spend more money on just one trip as opposed to doing three on a shoestring budget—simply put, quality over quantity. We worked with a travel agency to buy a fully-paid package that had all we wanted including our stay in five-star hotels and resorts for seven nights and eight days.

I had traveled several times to other countries on work assignments, but this was my first overseas trip with Anusha. We wanted to create great memories on this trip.

A chauffeur welcomed us at the Colombo airport; he was a Navy veteran. He spoke fluent English and was a warm gentleman with a loving family. Since we were on the road a lot that week, I was glad we had a well-groomed person to drive and act as a tour guide.

We had a blissful stay at the Taj Hotel in Colombo. I loved the spa experience. Anusha had never tried spa services. I had a hard time convincing her to try some experiences from the spa menu. Eventually, she agreed to try two from the long list of items on the menu. At the time, the family spa wasn't a thing yet, so we went to gender-specific rooms for treatment. I had some experience with body massage as part of my physical training, but this was heavenly. The ambiance, quality of service, and methodical work on relaxing through aroma, oil, body wraps, and heated-stone therapy were phenomenal. I thoroughly enjoyed every minute of it. Although it was familiar to me, for Anusha, this was a uniquely enchanting experience.

We both came out of our rooms after three hours, looking fresh and energized with peace written all over our faces. Even today I still remember the tranquility we enjoyed together, holding hands, and sharing our experiences.

Taj had several restaurants on the property, and we dined at a few of them for variety. We fell in love with the Chinese restaurant, going there for dinner three times during our stay! The luxurious experience was surreal—I never imagined the goodness of this trip.

We visited gardens, a tea estate, and temples and stayed in a special hotel in Nuwara Eliya, a former tea factory turned into a luxurious hotel.

It was a trip to remember. Although it was not Anusha's dream destination, she loved the rare luxury for one week. I was relieved that she enjoyed the trip too.

Without this goal on the list, I would not have ventured to spend a great deal of money on this trip. My goal was luxury travel. We experienced that and bottled wonderful memories and feelings over eight days.

This trip redefined "travel" for us. We both decided that less travel is acceptable, but when we *do* travel, we travel in style and plan ahead for the expenses, repeating the experience and adventure.

Time for reflection

- What's your dream vacation? Why?
- When can you fulfill this dream? What's needed?

"Travel and change of place impart new vigor to the mind." - *Seneca*

17

Running my first 10K

RACE

In 2009, I ran my first 10K race—at a time when I wasn't even ready for a 5K. I was fit, but not athletic. This was a moonshot goal for me. I used to walk or run on a treadmill three times a week for 20 minutes. I was focused on building muscles and maintaining my fitness at the time.

I met Gopal, a customs officer, at the gym. He was probably fifteen years older than me. We got along well. Gopal was passionate about running and was training for a 10K race that year.

He assured me I could walk during the race and I didn't have to run the whole distance. I thought this would be a good test for my fitness.

With Gopal as my training partner, I set a goal for my first 10K race in May 2009. This was my first ever racing event. Anusha did a 5K walk in the same event, her first time racing too.

Until I started training with Gopal, I had no idea how to train for distance races. I learned the basics of running and non-running workouts. I blindly followed his plan without knowing where it was leading me. On Sundays, we ran three miles (around 5 kilometers). That was beyond my aerobic capacity. It was exhausting and I felt sore until the next Sunday because I didn't know how to recover during non-running days. Still, I followed his plan for three months and prepared for the race. His plan was based on the wisdom gleaned from the internet!

Gopal was well-toned and in shape for the race. There were about 5,000 runners. I was surprised to see so many runners in the city. The energy and enthusiasm were palpable—just being there was a gift. Several runners had trained for months to be there and create personal records. I was in awe of some athlete's physiques and running strides near the start line.

Gopal and I started the race together. He had a good pace which I followed for the first two kilometers but was quickly drained of energy and became breathless. I asked him to continue as I started walking for the next 5 minutes. My plan was to walk the next two to three kilometers.

While walking, I was inspired to run and finish the race instead of continuing to walk. For some strange reason, I didn't want to walk that day. I don't know why. I knew I wasn't ready for that run, but I wanted to run the whole distance. That moment is unforgettable—even today, I can feel that moment of inspiration.

So, I started again, running slow but steady and not chasing anyone in my own pace and mental space. I crossed the 6K mark, which was the farthest I had run back then. I took a break at the next fuel station to hydrate and stretch. I decided to grit it and increase the speed for the next two kilometers.

Once I crossed the 7K mark, it was nearly impossible to run further. It's not realistic to run such a distance without proper training. My musculoskeletal structure wasn't ready for this level of demand. Aerobic capacity wasn't there either. Instead of risking quitting, I decided to walk the next ten to fifteen minutes. I'm glad I made that decision. I walked the next two kilometers and then decided to run the last kilometer. I felt a rush of energy in the last kilometer as I saw other runners sprinting and giving all they had to finish the race.

With the surge of energy, I gained a second wind—a fresh energy to run faster and finish strong.

Despite feeling sore, I ran faster than my starting pace and finished the race. I completed my first 10K in 75 minutes.

When I crossed the finish line, I was a different person. My level of consciousness elevated. There was a boost in my self-efficacy and belief in my athletic abilities. Crossing the finish line was a thrilling and memorable moment. It's an experience that cannot be explained in words—a word is not the thing—a feeling cannot be described in words. Like a sunset being described by a painter on the canvas is an impression, but not the sunset per se. It's the same with words to describe feelings.

That was the beginning of my passion for amateur running. I didn't participate in any athletic events in high school or college. I conveniently labeled myself as "academic," "nerd," and "bright." This event scratched the surface of the *athletic* side of me, a side that was never explored, nor nurtured. Right after the race, I decided to give more attention to training and come back stronger in the next year's race. That's how goals are; they are positively contagious. Goals have a domino effect.

TIME FOR REFLECTION

- Have you ever run a race?
- Are you open to attempting a 5K race this year?

"The reason we race isn't so much to beat each other ... but to be with each other." - Christopher McDougall

18

BEING A BUSINESS OWNER

I n 2010, Anusha and I started an internet distribution business. The biggest attraction of this business was personal development. It offered an exceptional quality leadership development program through recommended books, audio recordings, and conferences on a regular basis to help business owners become leaders. The products were great. There was no upfront investment, and it was definitely not a pyramid scheme. It did, however, make me realize the world of employment is actually a pyramid—the CEO always makes more money than all other employees and there can only be one CEO. Reflect on this for a few minutes and you'll realize it's 100 percent true. This was another reason for me to explore other avenues for earning income through my skills, experience, and passion. I wanted to own a business and this was an excellent opportunity in that direction.

I remember the day Anusha and I went to the first seminar where a couple stood on stage and spoke to a thousand people in a large conference hall. We were transported into the world of teamwork as a couple, setting goals and achieving them to realize our life dreams. For me, this was a lifetime opportunity to involve Anusha in the quest for self-development. The idea of reading books together, learning, and leading a business was fascinating.

Within the first six weeks, we realized it was a people business. Without people skills and integrity, there was no business. We also discovered our own personality styles, execution quirks, and discipline issues along the way. But we were fast learners and had amazing mentors to support us. In front of our leaders, we openly shared our challenges and started holding ourselves accountable as a couple—as one entity—as a business. In the process of building the business, we also built ourselves and a strong foundation of togetherness. We are forever grateful to two couples for their guidance and support: Rajan Warrier and Prabha Warrier, and R Balakrishnan and Veni.

Our personal growth was a blessing in the process, in addition to growing the business we continued expanding our thinking. Our family members were supportive and they did a good job hiding their perceptions—they actually thought we were crazy to pursue this with gusto and drive. They didn't see what we saw and we understood that. For us, money was not the goal, it was a byproduct of becoming the best version of us.

At large conventions, we met successful couples who were doctors, accountants, engineers, and entrepreneurs. They were already successful in their lives yet were passionately building their distribution business. We clearly knew what motivated them—significance. They had already achieved success. Now they were searching for significance. That's not easy to comprehend, let alone appreciate.

For us, it was a journey of entrepreneurship—strategy, goals, plan, execution, leadership, and working with people— skills that are invaluable for entrepreneurs.

My passion for training, coaching, and developing leaders increased tenfold during those years. I became a better manager, trainer, and coach. I had the opportunity to listen to hundreds of international speakers and keynote speeches—so much learning and growth.

We achieved several goals in the business, the most important one was *being a business owner*. We learned to appreciate our differences and complement each other through our innate strengths. Our mindset changed. A change in mindset is priceless. We cannot put a price tag on the implications of that change.

TIME FOR REFLECTION

- What kind of business would you like to own? When can you start?
- Which skills are necessary to launch your business, and who could assist you with them?

"Whenever you see a successful business, someone once made a courageous decision." - Peter F. Drucker

19

Shaping personality through Benjamin Franklin's method

What if you could wear your personality like a jacket? Choose any attribute you like and wear it. What if you could choose to be confident, humble, or assertive? Turns out we can gain any virtue we want and add it to our being. After all, we are creatures of habit, and we can build new habits.

I read this idea in a book, *The Autobiography of Benjamin Franklin*. Ben Franklin decided on 13 virtues that he deemed valuable to inculcate into his being. He then practiced one virtue for a week. Each week, he would pick a virtue from his list and deliberately demonstrate it in his daily interactions. After 13 weeks, he repeated the process, starting again with item number one on the list. This means he completed four cycles every year over the course of 52 weeks. What a creative way to build new virtues! I set a goal to attempt this for two years.

The idea was fascinating. If it worked for Ben Franklin, it would work for anyone, including me—especially me, since I needed to change. Several things needed to change within me. Being assertive was my weakest link—I never said no to people. Lack of assertiveness caused stress while I was running a distribution business, which I discussed in the previous chapter.

Through self-reflection and discussions with my mentors, I became aware of my default orientation to life: people-pleasing. I didn't know any better. I vacillated between two extremes, submission or aggression. Being in the middle, being assertive, was the missing link. In fact, I see the same link missing in many of my clients. People pleasing sucks energy out of us. It makes us spineless. Ben Franklin's method was a practical way to strengthen the spine, one behavior at a time!

I wrote my list of seven virtues. They dealt with people and life situations. I wrote them on the back of business cards in my Rolodex (It's a great use of business cards—collect them.). Seven cards with clearly written virtues along with short precepts describing them. I would pick one card for each week and keep it with me throughout the day.

The first thing I did after I woke up was read that week's card and reflect on why it mattered to me, followed by how I could demonstrate it during the day at home, my workplace, and in other interactions with people.

During breaks and lunchtime, I pulled out the card from my pocket for a 30-second reflection. To ensure I was putting theory into practice, this reminder nudged me in the right direction. If I had not shown any changes by lunchtime, then I would redouble my effort and be more conscious of opportunities to deploy the day's virtue. Initially, it was weird, but later this started working. I deliberately indulged in new behaviors as weeks went by. I started changing.

With this virtue-building technique, I added seven behaviors to my personality: smiling more, talking to strangers, listening with interest, asking questions, respectfully disagreeing, providing critical feedback, and saying *no*. I don't carry cards anymore, but I still practice it mentally. See the power of habit?

Incorporating new behaviors can be fun. Don't make it all about "thinking." That'll never get you to your destination. Focus on "doing," and soon enough, you'll get to "living" the virtues. It's the action that leads to transformation, not information. Making it a game will help. For example, you could gamify it. Talking to three strangers every day is a great goal. It's not complicated. It's just a short exchange of comments or compliments. It may seem daunting at first, but once you give it a try, you'll find it enjoyable. You don't need to be good to start, but you need to start to be good!

Through this goal, I worked on myself and practiced these seven virtues for two years. Over the years, I have added many more virtues to my being using this technique. Conscious behavioral change is fun.

TIME FOR REFLECTION

- What character traits or behaviors would you like to develop?
- Which traits would you remove from your personality, and when could you start?

"Without continual growth and progress, such words as improvement, achievement, and success have no meaning." - *Benjamin Franklin*

Benjamin Franklin's 13 virtues: Temperance, Silence, Order, Resolution, Frugality, Industry, Sincerity, Justice, Moderation, Cleanliness, Tranquility, Chastity, and Humility.

20

ACHIEVING AN UNWRITTEN GOAL

S ometimes you don't need a formal goal. A strong intention can bring synchronicity and serendipity in your life. During Anusha's pregnancy, we kept talking about how I would be with her during the time of delivery. In India, this practice was not common in many hospitals at that time. Few hospitals allowed partners to be in the delivery room, nevertheless, we both strongly wanted this in our lives.

We talked to Anusha's doctor several times during our visits. The doctor was supportive, yet she couldn't guarantee us this would happen due to several constraints. At least, she assured us she would consider our request and talk about it when the day arrived.

A week before the projected date, Anusha felt discomfort and we rushed to the hospital. The doctor promptly examined Anusha and determined that it was an urgent situation requiring immediate attention. Anusha required a C-section operation to ensure the safety and health of the baby. We couldn't afford to wait another week for a normal delivery.

It was the fifth of September, celebrated as Teachers' Day in India. We rushed to the operating theater. The doctor was a bit worried about the situation. I could see the concern on her face, which in turn, alarmed me. She enlisted her mentor, an expert gynecologist, to join her for the procedure. I'm so grateful to our doctor who knew her limitations and truly cared for Anusha.

I was asked to wait outside the operating room. Our doctor said, "Sorry Pramoda, this is a complex situation and we won't be able to let you witness this surgery." Anusha and I both felt sad. This is precisely the time a couple wants to be together—more so because of the complication and uncertainty. Reluctantly, we agreed, and I waited outside, waving goodbye as I stayed near the door. The doors closed slowly, and worrisome thoughts began to open in my mind.

In a few minutes, Anusha's parents joined the scene. I was pacing in the hallway, praying and hoping for Anusha and the baby's health and safety. The chief doctor of the hospital was walking into the room. He said, "This case needs me to be in the room, so I am here to offer guidance to other doctors." I thanked him. He then asked me, "Would you like to come inside and witness the process? Not everyone can do this, so let me know if you're up for this adventure."

I couldn't believe what he said. Feeling goosebumps on my arms and neck, I said *yes* and walked in with him.

I entered the room wearing a surgical gown, fully covered in blue. I was on Anusha's left side and held her left hand while stroking her forehead. The anesthetic drug was not fully in effect. She could see me and talk to me. She was relieved to see me next to her. I saw her face change once she realized we were together. I don't think she remembers these details, but I remember it like it happened yesterday.

There was a green screen that covered her chest and below. She couldn't see what was happening. After twenty-five minutes, the baby popped out of her belly. The doctors slowly pushed the baby out and I could see all that from where I was standing. The pediatrician cut the umbilical cord, cleaned the baby, and announced, "It's a boy." In India, parents know the gender of the child only after birth.

We can call it a coincidence, serendipity, or synchronicity. The fact is that our strong desire to be together during Samyak's birth was a magical reality. It was an unwritten goal, yet we ended up achieving it.

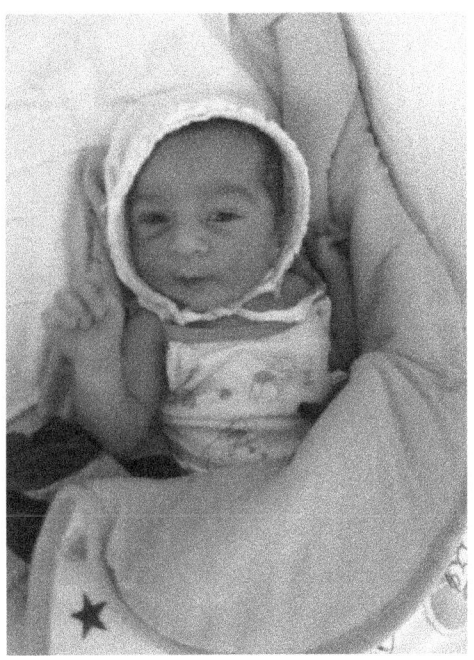

TIME FOR REFLECTION

- Have you achieved goals in your life without formally writing them?
- If yes, was it due to your burning desire to achieve them? How can you fan the flame of desire toward other important goals?

"Our intention creates our reality." - *Wayne W. Dyer*

21

REACHING A 90-DAY YOGA STREAK

I wasn't always comfortable waking up early. Waking up early was a one step forward and two steps backward situation for me. I couldn't maintain consistency and motivation in this area until I read the book *The 5 AM Club* by Robin Sharma. The author convinced me to consider waking up early and owning my mornings. I was ready to start this journey. I was looking for a goal to latch on to.

An opportunity knocked on my door. Anusha had been going to yoga classes at 6:00 a.m. I thought this was a chance for me to join her and attempt waking up a bit earlier. I woke up at seven for years, so my plan was to wake up before six first and then aim for 5:00 a.m. after a few months. The other objective I wanted to accomplish was to explore group yoga classes. Since my body was flexible, I didn't think yoga would help me much in toning—or so I thought. We gather beliefs on our way through life like small wires wrought into strong cables. Luckily, I was open to trying. This openness swings wide the door to possibilities.

My goal was to show up for ninety days without fail and attend the 6:00 a.m. class. I wasn't focused on any outcome. It was all about the practice and the process.

I enjoyed guided yoga postures and breathing exercises. Our teacher was well-versed in headstand posture. She did it with ease and grace. I thought it was a good stretch goal for me in this process of learning.

I started following her instructions, stretching myself little by little, and kept practicing over a few weeks. In a month's time, I was doing headstands without the wall support. This was unbelievable! I thought it was out of my range, but it happened in less than a month. I showed up consistently and did the work.

My mind used to race during the practice sessions, impeding the balance and grace of the postures. Though I realized it, I didn't put much effort into it. Looking back now, I see how the state of mind impacts the strength, quality, and grace of yoga postures. When the mind is not revved up, getting into a tough posture seems easy and doable. Our mind is like a snow globe. We need to keep it still and let our thoughts settle by gently noticing them.

I continued to attend classes for more than five months, well beyond the original goal of three months. Those five months of consistent behaviors changed two of my wrong beliefs: first, I feel uncomfortable getting up early, and second, yoga doesn't help my body type.

This experience busted those old beliefs. I realized I *can* wake up earlier than 7:00 a.m. and yoga indeed helps all body types. This made me ponder, what other beliefs can be questioned? Such a line of inquiry opens Pandora's box of limiting beliefs.

I achieved my goal and started waking before 6:00 a.m. through this proxy goal of a 90-day streak in yoga classes. After five months of doing this, it became a habit.

TIME FOR REFLECTION

- What new habits would you like to develop?
- How can you start your streak from today?

"A mind free from all disturbances is yoga." - Patanjali

22

BECOMING A WORKSHOP FACILITATOR AT ORACLE

If you remember my story from a previous chapter, I had tried making additional income as a social skill and leadership facilitator. I wanted to level up this experiment with my training modules as an independent consultant. There was one hurdle—getting consent from Oracle for doing this as a side hustle. I approached the HR in India and I sensed reluctance and resistance from them. Back then, it was a strange request from an engineering leader. I'm sure they didn't know how to respond since I was blazing a new trail. I then talked to my manager Bence Gazdag. He was fully supportive and asked me to talk to the VP of the organization, Sue Locke, who was based in the UK.

Sue was thrilled about my goal and was super supportive. She offered one idea to polish my proposal. Sue asked me to conduct the same workshops at Oracle, *free of charge*, for individuals interested in attending. This was a brilliant idea. It had never crossed my mind. That's why I love talking to people about goals; I get a different perspective and it's helpful. When I wrote the proposal I mentioned the types of training modules, details about no conflict-of-interest, and how I can help other employees in the organization without incurring additional cost. I clarified my consulting hours and declared that all moonlighting work would be during non-office hours and weekends.

The proposal was approved after weeks of deliberation. As a result, I was officially cleared to engage in training activities for monetary benefits. This was a milestone to remember—a goal to celebrate. I could spend all my energy on building more modules and helping the organization while advancing my own pursuit of happiness and excitement—a true win-win situation.

I already had a couple of modules I prepared for members of the Toastmasters club. I polished them further to create two full-day modules. They were "Time Management" and "Public Speaking." I later added other modules: "Working with People," "Know Your Personality," "Questions are the Answers," and "Coaching Skills for Managers."

It was evident that I loved creating communication and leadership courses. I was like a kid in a candy store. I loved the experience of creating content–every bit of it: identifying leadership gaps, interviewing people, doing research, reading books, and creating courses that enabled transformation in people. I added moderated exercises, self-reflection, and group sharing to all my courses.

People gave rave reviews on my courses to their managers. I did two sessions every month at Oracle. There were fifteen to twenty people in each workshop. They came from several departments while the news spread by word-of-mouth. Several managers and directors attended my workshops. They loved the sessions and left glowing reviews for content, engagement, and delivery.

I also experimented with other audiences: hotel staff, small business teams, MBA students, and so on. I really enjoyed all the interactions and opportunities to meet people, understand their challenges, and help them with my experience and insights.

None of this would have happened without a goal to begin with. With a goal, a lot happened. I created opportunities by enlisting support from mentors and guides. I was relentless. I was process-oriented. I put in a ton of effort. Most importantly, I enjoyed the journey. Every time I share my knowledge with an audience, I find meaning and purpose. The meaning draws me to this activity of sharing wisdom.

TIME FOR REFLECTION

- What new challenges are you ready to take on in your profession?
- What if you sought out stretch assignments in your current job? Who could help?

"Your diamonds are not in far distant mountains or in yonder seas; they are in your own backyard if you but dig for them." - Russell Conwell

23

CONDUCTING MY FIRST
PUBLIC SEMINAR

Most of my workshops followed a pattern where all participants came from a single organization. This held true for training sessions conducted at Oracle as well as those organized for other external organizations (as a freelance trainer). I wanted to facilitate all-day workshops where people from diverse backgrounds could come and learn together. A public program that could be open to anyone interested. A cohort of learners from disparate backgrounds.

This goal needed a radically different strategy: identifying the audience, reaching them, and showing the transformation to bring them under one roof for a seminar. It was an exciting challenge for me and I went for it. Working in a marketing technology organization, I was familiar with lead generation strategies and the available tactics for perfect execution.

My strategy included social media, email marketing, talking to my network, and seeking referrals. I also enlisted support from my friend Srikanthan Kumarasamy, who had held leadership roles at Microsoft. At the time, he was a full-time coach and entrepreneur. I invited him to join as a co-facilitator in this workshop.

We called the workshop "The Mind Game of Leadership." It was an attempt to introduce three leadership frameworks to increase awareness and equip participants with practical tools for demonstrating leadership behaviors in their roles. Our approach was to address the mindset and establish mindful behaviors for effective leadership.

I worked with an agency that had a few hundred thousand emails of potential candidates in Bengaluru. Our goal was an in-person workshop; online teaching wasn't popular back in the day.

When we sent an email blast on a Monday, the response was overwhelming. People responded to our email and called me on my cell phone to learn more details. Handling those calls, understanding the audience's needs, and answering questions on pricing were great skills I picked up by doing rather than reading. It was a classic story of "ready, fire, and aim."

I gathered these during our experience with the internet distribution business. All the skills that an entrepreneur needs were already in my being—they just flowed naturally in this adventure.

Some calls were made by other trainers in the city who wanted to know more about the facilitators, since we weren't popular names yet in the circuit. One trainer even questioned my experience and credibility. I had to explain my background and corporate tenure, and I had to back my claim in marketing emails.

For some, it's critical to have the credentials to appreciate other people—some sort of organizational or educational institution seal. I had the seal but chose not to leverage my employer in these marketing emails.

This was a crucible for my belief and authenticity. When you have substance, you can handle any question about what you're offering. Without the substance, the form is fragile. Such calls also underscored the need for my website and presence on social media. Since I was moonlighting as a facilitator, these aspects were completely out of my radar. It was an experiment and I was learning a lot. All experiments bring success because they test what's possible without looking for specific outcomes.

Eight weeks of focused effort attracted about twelve participants who paid for the workshop. I allowed five people (friends and co-workers from Oracle) at no cost to attend the full-day event. The session was on a Saturday, in a hotel conference room. It was a grand success.

I had pulled off a day-long workshop with seventeen people on a weekend. I had proved this could work for me. After this experience, I was a facilitator who could run open workshops. This was the beginning of designing cohort-based courses on leadership development.

TIME FOR REFLECTION

- What constitutes your career capital, that is, your rare and valuable skills?
- Who would pay you for sharing your knowledge or expertise? Can you run some tests?

"Experiments never fail." - Dale Dauten

According to Cal Newport, a computer science professor and author well-known for his books on work and productivity, *career capital* refers to the unique skills and abilities that make you valuable and irreplaceable in the job market. Newport's concept of career capital is a central theme in his book *So Good They Can't Ignore You*, where he argues against the common advice to "follow your passion" and instead suggests that building valuable skills (career capital) is the key to finding work you love.

24

OWNING A PENTHOUSE

I'd like to talk about one goal that wasn't originally mine and still ended up being achieved. I purchased a house in 2007, before getting married. Anusha's dream was bigger in this area, perhaps even better. Owning things was never a priority for me. She wanted a better place to live and she went after it. It was a penthouse in an apartment complex.

Anusha did all the research and then took me on a tour of the property. At first, the goal seemed far-fetched to me. I didn't want to go for it, but I melted in the fire of her desire. In no time, it became a joint dream, and we were a dream team!

We planned for several weeks to arrange the initial payment and crafted a strategy for future monthly payments. Our experience was like driving a car in the night with headlights on, we could see one hundred feet ahead of us. As we went further, we saw the next hundred feet. It was a crazy ride for a few months until we signed the paper and officially got the sale agreement in our hands.

This was a time in my life when I was drawn by someone else's goal. I just followed Anusha and supported her in this journey. Sharing our concerns, fears, and perspectives openly also strengthened our relationship. Each discussion made us open up and discuss freely, adding another layer of trust and love. I still joke with her about this property—without her, we would never have purchased that house. Absolutely no way, period!

It happened because Anusha had a strong goal, and together we achieved it. Just like a company thrives because of a leader's vision, a family can thrive with one person's vision. The other person can join the movement when momentum picks up. This works as long as the other person doesn't throw wrenches into the wheel of progression. That's all we need.

Here's the fun part. We bought that house with so much passion and we have never lived there!

The house was ready after we moved to the United States. Someone else has been living there for years as a tenant, but we have no regrets. We learned a lot in the process. We became better individuals—more understanding and more patient with each other. That's more valuable than the experience of living in that house. What we became in the process is priceless.

This episode is a classic example of how goals can be achieved with a burning desire and massive consistent action. With these two in place, goals become reality. Full effort is full victory. When we leave no stone unturned in pursuit of an objective, miracles can and do happen.

While pursuing goals, we cross the threshold of our thinking. We go beyond our perceived limits. We become unstoppable. People sense that spirit. With such a spirit, you can show up fully inspired and engaged. You can turn foes into supporters, doubters to fans, and strangers to friends.

I'm not preaching here. I have seen this happen many times with goals in general, and specifically with this goal. We have marveled at how things shaped up throughout the entire process—from the seeds of the dream to the fruits of its realization.

TIME FOR REFLECTION

- Is there any goal your partner (or spouse) wants to pursue to which you're not ready to commit?
- What if you trusted their instincts and supported them wholeheartedly?

"When you want something, all the universe conspires in helping you to achieve it." - Paulo Coelho

25

Prioritizing family time

Two years after Samyak was born, Anusha and I realized we needed more juice in our lives. She was on a career break. She was a full-time mom and I was busy during weekdays, resulting in very little face time on weekdays. We didn't want to live on weekends exclusively; life is lived every day. Every day counts; there are seven days in a week.

We went out for a brainstorming session. Our favorite place for brainstorming is coffee shops. We started with Coffee Day and then fell in love with Starbucks' ambiance— for us it's a place for reflection, sharing, and dreaming.

I remember the discussion like it happened an hour ago. It was three in the afternoon. We took a paper napkin and listed things that brought us joy. We talked about planning well and intentionally injecting these "acts of joy" into our daily routine. Several themes emerged from that napkin (several napkins to be precise). Having quality time with Samyak, time for us, and connection with extended family. I'll highlight three things here to underscore the specificity of the changes we committed to make.

First, the two of us agreed to meet at Starbucks once a week to talk, share, and review our commitments. This was a breakthrough in our relationship, a higher level of commitment. We didn't use the phone, nor bring our laptops—we just talked and listened to each other. It was a new experience. We enjoyed every moment of it and looked forward to our coffee dates every week. It became an outlet for us to share feelings, seek support, and help each other become a better version of ourselves. It became a positive ritual in our relationship.

Second, we decided to go out for dinner every Wednesday as a family. It was a Kerala-style Ayurvedic restaurant managed by the Art of Living organization in Bengaluru. We were in love with the serenity of this place. We went there with Samyak. At times we also took along my mother, Anusha's parents, or both. All have great memories attached to this place. We went every Wednesday, for more than 12 months.

And lastly, we went to the swimming pool in our apartment complex three times a week. Sometimes we picked a weekday, to break the pattern and avoid getting consumed with my work commitments. I walked in the pool carrying Samyak in my arms or played with him while he floated in his life jacket. Anusha would either be in the pool or relaxing on a lawn chair reading a book. It was a wonderful family time and we created those time blocks deliberately.

Sitting in coffee shops, offering undivided attention, and openly sharing our feelings became a permanent part of our relationship. Supporting, coaching, challenging, and sometimes simply being there—we wore several hats in those meetings. This one change made a lasting impact on our relationship. It's one of those things that completely shifts your perspective in life and continues to become a part of you.

As a couple, we have worked really hard on ourselves and our relationship. It's a lifelong endeavor. We are a team; we recommit to the team spirit through these coffee dates.

The quote below from Leo Buscaglia serves as an inspiration and an ideal for us. [4]

"As soon as the love relationship does not lead me to me, as soon as I in a love relationship do not lead another person to himself, this love, even if it seems to be the most secure and ecstatic attachment I have ever experienced, is not true love. For real love is dedicated to continual becoming."

TIME FOR REFLECTION

- What do you enjoy doing with your family and loved ones?
- How can you adjust your schedule to allow for more family time?

"We are trained to analyze problems and create solutions. We forget that marriage is a relationship, not a project to be completed or a problem to solve." - Gary Chapman

---

4   Leo F. Buscaglia, *Love* (Ballantine Books, 1996)

26

RUNNING MY FIRST HALF MARATHON

Four years after I ran my first 10K race, I registered for a half marathon in 2013. I was at a stage where I ran 10K every weekend to stay in shape and maintain my aerobic capacity. Like any distance runner, the next step for me was to run a half marathon (13 miles or 21 kilometers). Doubling this distance is not easy, especially crossing the mental chasm. I attempted to run 15K once on a Sunday. It was tough and I couldn't run beyond 12 kilometers. It was obvious that I needed more muscle strength. I invested a few months to build strength and endurance; I didn't want to rush.

Many of my friends in the running circuit had already graduated to half and full marathons. Since I competed with my best version, I didn't feel left out, and I didn't compare with anyone. We are all running against our own limited thinking, challenging our perceived limits, and pushing the envelope. In this process, others' success should trigger inspiration, not frustration. Comparison is toxic. It's the thief of joy.

Filled with doubt and fear of injury, I signed up for a half marathon. My strategy was to finish the race by walking the last five or six kilometers if I found it difficult to run. This was an acceptable goal—finishing and crossing the finish line with a sense of accomplishment.

When the distance is greater, runners tend to pace and conserve energy. My focus was to conserve energy and see how long I could continue my stride on the course. I started slow and managed to complete the first 10K in sixty-five minutes. I took a break at the fuel station to stretch and assess my body's battery.

I slowed down further, considering the remaining distance of eleven more kilometers. Thoughts swarmed like mosquitoes in my head, seeking reasons to quit the race and not push beyond my limit. I continued while the music of the mind kept playing. I just focused on one step at a time and kept going.

When I crossed the fourteen-kilometer mark, a thought struck me. "This is the longest distance I have ever run in my life. I didn't walk so far. I could do this—if only I keep this pace and don't rush to jeopardize my chances."

There was a sense of relief, a slow rising of fresh energy in me. I had heard about the "second wind" of runners but had never experienced it before, so I wasn't sure about what that experience meant.

I crossed the sixteen-kilometer mark—only five more to go. There were no pangs of pain or discomfort; it was a surreal feeling. The run felt effortless as if the wind was helping me from behind, pushing me to finish this race. With the feeling of wind on my back, I increased my pace to test if I could run faster and finish sooner. Doubts were replaced with certainty, I knew I would finish this race, without walking—I had run the whole time.

At the twentieth kilometer, I decided to sprint the last kilometer and give every ounce of energy left in me. I was smiling, feeling victorious, and joyful like a kid running back home after school. There was no sense of pain, no doubt, no fear. I was in the "zone"—a state of flow—a thought-free moment.

I crossed the finish line with a dash at the end completing the race in two hours and thirteen minutes. I had achieved a new goal! I had crossed the threshold of my own thinking. I experienced a newfound confidence, belief, and certainty. I was transformed, breaking through the limitations of my mind and doubling the race distance from 10 kilometers to 21 kilometers.

TIME FOR REFLECTION

- If you have already run a 5K or 10K race, are you ready for a half marathon?
- If running is not your thing, how can you increase your physical activity?

"There are no limitations to the mind except those we acknowledge." - Napoleon Hill

27

Studying J Krishnamurti

"*I*t is no measure of health to be well adjusted to a profoundly sick society." - J Krishnamurti

I was blown away by this quote when I read it in an online article. The quote was piercing, and full of meaning. I hadn't heard of J Krishnamurti, more popularly known as K among his followers. I learned about J Krishnamurti from a friend whom I met in a coach training program. Being a student of self-help, naturally, I became inquisitive about K. If you listen to his speeches on YouTube, you'll be surprised at his level of consciousness. Clearly, he was ahead of his time and that's palpable when you listen to his talks.

His talk "The Network of Thought" gives a small taste of his medicine. Like all medicine, what he says may not be sweet. K challenges your perceptions. He's direct, intense, and a force of nature. Inspired by his talks, I set a goal to study his work.

There is an international school in Bengaluru which is run by the Krishnamurti Foundation. I attended their monthly meeting one Sunday. I participated in their group discussions (called dialogues), mostly listening and trying to understand the essence of K's teaching. It was intriguing, but there was no method or process to raise awareness.

I appreciated K's spirit and intensity in his writing and recorded lectures, but I couldn't quite put my finger on how this could be applied to my life. During his lifetime, K went around the world giving lectures on various topics for over five decades. Most of his talks are available as books. Many of these talks are available on YouTube.

I started visiting the study center more often to read these books and watch the video lectures on weekends. Sometimes I went alone; Anusha joined me a few times.

One Sunday, Anusha and I watched a video talk named "Relationship is a Mirror." I still remember the day. It was just the two of us watching a large screen. K talked about how we can see ourselves in a relationship. It's a mirror showing our true selves. He then talked about how past memories impact relationships and we meet people in the past, not in the present. We relate with images from past interactions and we react to those formed images. It was an intriguing and engaging talk.

I continued to read books and listen to his speeches. Even though it looked cryptic in the beginning, I began understanding and experiencing a sense of calm through repeated exposure to his philosophy. The more I immersed myself in his ideas, the better I was able to observe the dynamics of my own thoughts. K's teachings helped me understand the power of thought—nurturing the observer in me.

I attended a three-day retreat to learn more about his teachings. During this time, I read his journal entries, where K shared his thoughts on various aspects of life. His journals were a window into his soul and consciousness. Little did I know how much all of this would help me and my coaching clients. We're creatures of thought; we're wrought in thought like a giant cable made of millions of tiny wires.

If you're keen to learn about K's teachings, start with videos on YouTube. His dialogues with Dr. David Bohm and Dr. Shainberg are my all-time favorites. K asks questions to

Dr. Shainberg in those interviews. As a listener, you'll feel as if those questions are thrown at you like curve balls.

"Thought is a response to memory. Fear is a thought," said K in his talks.

If you enjoy reading books, I recommend starting with these two: *Think on These Things* and *Total Freedom*. You can dip your toes into them first before delving deep into exploring the depth of his message.

With this goal, I studied Krishnamurti's work for more than two years. Even today, on long drives, I occasionally listen to his talks. Samyak appreciates K's speaking style, while we admire the substance of what he says.

TIME FOR REFLECTION

- Who is your favorite philosopher, and what aspects of their philosophy do you appreciate?
- How can you invest time this year to study more about them and their work?

"The function of philosophy is to teach us to think, not what to think." - Voltaire

The word *philosophy* has its roots in ancient Greek. It is derived from the Greek words *philos*, meaning "love," and *sophia*, meaning "wisdom or knowledge." Thus, the literal meaning of philosophy is "love of wisdom or the pursuit of knowledge."

28

TRAINING AS A COACH

In 2013, I had six years of experience in training and facilitating group workshops. I didn't think of extending the arc to one-on-one coaching until 2014 when I signed up for a coach training program. I had the experience of working with a coach, but I never thought of *being* a coach. My friend and mentor Srikanthan Kumarasamy had signed up and he insisted that I do as well. It's wonderful to have mentors who look out for you. You'll encounter new opportunities when you have a supportive network of people who care about your personal growth.

The program included 100 hours of educational sessions, one-on-one, and proctored peer coaching. There were twenty other people in this program. I was the youngest in the group.

I had read a couple of books on coaching before this program. The course curriculum piqued my curiosity. I made a list of books that I wanted to study. Some of them were recommended books in the course and some I added based on my interest and inclination to know specific areas in more detail.

The list had fifty books! I had never read fifty books in twelve months. That year, 2014, was a year of personal development. I chose 50 books to read and invested sixty minutes every day—sometimes more than two hours.

Regardless of what happened, I clocked 60 minutes of reading every day for 12 months. I had an international trip that year and I squeezed every extra minute I had in my hotel room or airplane to soak in the wisdom of various authors.

The results were evident. I showed up with enthusiasm and energy in peer coaching sessions. I asked insightful questions, and I improved my listening skills. I came across as an experienced coach since I did the work before the coaching sessions. I devoured books on Neuro-Linguistic Programming (NLP). The book *Structure of Magic* became my playbook for coaching conversations.

Core ideas of NLP became part of my being and thinking, as well as tools for self-awareness—especially awareness of language. Words paint our experience, and I realized the power of words. When I say, "I spent an hour reading a book" versus "I invested an hour reading a book," there's a difference. The difference is subtle and it makes all the difference in our perception.

Naturally, all the skills I gathered through my coach training program helped me become a better leader at work and bring higher accountability to my team to deliver results. Personal growth affects all areas of our lives, like sunlight spreading across the ocean.

I applied all my education that year in coaching conversations. We had proctored coaching conversations during this program. I *loved* this part! I enjoyed being observed by fifteen other people while engaging in a coaching conversation. It was a perfect opportunity to hone the craft of coaching.

With all this effort, personal growth, and passion, I became a trained coach in October 2014 after nine months.

During a one-on-one coaching session, master coach Ram Ramanathan, who led the program, appreciated my efforts and my thirst to hone the craft as a coach. He recommended that I sign up for a 10-day silence meditation course called Vipassana. Ram said the silence meditation would help me in two ways: first, by improving my listening skills during coaching conversations, and second, by helping me understand my own mental drama through observing my thoughts and self-talk. Convinced by these two benefits, I added this course to my list of goals.

TIME FOR REFLECTION

- What adjacent opportunities can you create based on your career capital?
- How could you help others in your industry as a coach or mentor?

"Coaching is unlocking people's potential to maximize their own performance." - *Sir John Whitmore*

29

ENJOYING 10 DAYS OF
SILENCE

In 2014, I decided to attend a Vipassana meditation course after my coach and mentor Ram Ramanthan recommended it to me. Upon researching this course, my excitement turned into fear. Ten days of silence, 10 hours of sitting meditation, waking at 4:00 a.m. every day, no access to phone, laptop, books, or notepad—a life in true solitude. You and your thoughts for ten days. No one else is allowed to interact with you. Essentially, you live as a *monk* during the course. The description seemed daunting. Taking ten days off from work and family priorities for a personal goal was another hurdle to cross.

I discussed this with Anusha and planned to attend a course after six months. She wondered if I could do this. I explained this goal to her and how it would benefit me both personally and professionally as a coach. She's a sweetheart; she's always supportive toward my goals. Samyak was a toddler at the time, and those ten days would be challenging for her. Luckily, my in-laws were there to support Anusha.

Before signing up I also communicated this to my team and stakeholders at work to ensure there was no reason to back out at any cost. I managed a large organization at the time.

Anusha dropped me off at the center on the designated day. By 6:00 p.m., I deposited all my personal items in a locker. The main gates of the premises were locked. I felt like a prisoner at that moment. Technically, we are all prisoners of our minds—there's no greater prison than this. It holds us until we die.

The first three days were extremely difficult. Watching my breath going in and out through my nose for ten hours a day was exhausting. I wondered if I could get out of this sooner than ten days. I started counting the days. I was growing restless. I wasn't aware of my thoughts; they had free rein. My mind was like a shaken snow globe—agitated and restless.

After the fourth day, I started realizing the pull of thoughts. My thoughts wandered all over. One minute I was in my high school days and the next minute I would fantasize about my adventure after ten days of silence. I was never in the present moment. I was indeed absent in the present. This awareness itself was a remarkable insight. I wanted to deepen this awareness, which inspired me to stop counting the days and start being fully present in the program.

After six days, I started enjoying the hour-long meditation sessions. I was no longer restless. I wasn't chasing my thoughts. The snow globe was not in a shaken state. I was able to notice my thoughts and come back to the present moment. I realized that every time I noticed a thought, I was developing mindfulness, that was an *indicator* of progress. Each session was 60 minutes long. Opening my eyes after hearing a loud gong was a unique feeling. It's not easy to stay in one place with closed eyes that long—that too for *ten* hours a day!

What I picked up from the course is the experience of a *meditative state*. The state is more important than the practice. Practice helps us go back to that state. To me, what's most useful is being in this state during difficult life situations, especially when things don't go according to my expectations. That's when the rubber meets the road. Without this realization, all the effort is in vain. It's like showing heavy dumbbells in my home gym, but not using them to build my muscles. Dumbbells have no value unless I lift them.

With a meditation practice, we build our *responsive* muscles and become less *reactive*. We do this by resisting the random pull of thoughts and staying in the present.

One research scientist said, "Meditation is like brushing your brain." When you brush your teeth, do you say, "It was deep," or proudly announce, "Today was better than yesterday," or any such commentary? No, of course not!

So the same thing applies to meditation practice. We do it to reconnect and identify with the sky, to disengage from our thought clouds—to be in the moment, to be present here and now—not catching the next train of thought. More importantly, it is continuing to stay in the mindful state when life throws curve balls at us.

The Vipassana 10-day meditation course made a significant impact on my life. I highly recommend you attempt one course and experience it for yourself. You'll thank me for this strong recommendation. I went back after five years, in 2019, *for another 10-day course.*

TIME FOR REFLECTION

- Do you have a meditation practice? If not, could you start with 5 to 10 minutes once a day?
- Are you open to attending a 10-day Vipassana course to get in touch with your inner/true self?

"Anything that arises in the mind will manifest itself as a sensation on the body; if you observe this sensation, you are observing both the mind as well as matter." - S. N. Goenka

The term *Vipassana* originates from the Pali language, which is a language closely related to Sanskrit and is used in the Theravada Buddhist tradition. The word *Vipassana* is composed of two parts:

- *Vi* means "special or distinct."
- *Passana* comes from the Pali verb "passati," which means "to see, to observe, or to perceive."

When combined, *Vipassana* can be translated as "clear seeing, insight, or introspective vision."

30

ORGANIZING A BLOOD DONATION CAMP

With Anusha's support, I set a goal to organize a blood donation camp in January 2015. Through this event, we wanted to give an opportunity to our friends and family to donate blood. I had donated twenty-three times before this event in my quest of "donating blood 50 times before 50." I worked with a blood bank to find a venue and plan logistics. Our goal was to collect 50 units that day. The goal looked beyond reach. That didn't deter us, we were ready to do what was needed.

For three weeks, we went around enlisting people and sharing the event details. About 10 people expressed interest and some were committed to participating in the event no matter what.

The event started at 10:00 a.m. I was the first donor that day followed by Anusha and a couple of other folks. By 1:00 p.m. we had 10 donors—pre-registered and walk-ins included. We had three more hours left. I started thinking about how we were short of our original goal. But I also knew the power of strong goals and the effort invested in the days leading to the event. I waited there with a glimmer of hope. As an organizer that's a tough situation since the blood bank invests one full day for such events. So, their time and effort were at stake as well.

After 2:00 p.m., more people started showing up. Some were friends of friends who had registered. Some were strangers who saw the event banner and walked in. Some dragged their friends or relatives to this event. The event was at a language school in Bengaluru. One teacher brought her students above age 18 to check their eligibility for donation. Two of them were eligible, based on weight and hemoglobin level. It was their *first* donation.

It was an unusual experience to see so many unregistered participants walking in to donate blood out of nowhere. Donors made phone calls to their friends to invite them after they donated. It was all magical. The turn of events was unbelievable. The count was 26 units by 4 p.m. Our original goal was 50, but we finally ended the camp by collecting 26 units. That was my twenty-fourth donation.

This is yet another example of how goals can shape outcomes. By choosing to walk in a direction and sticking to the path, we inspire others to follow us. Passion inspires people, serving motivates them, and *service alters the suffering self!*

Several participants had no idea what blood donation entailed. They experienced it for the first time; they felt wonderful being in selfless service to others. Blood donation involves giving a portion of what's in your body to help someone else.

I remember the look on their faces when they saw their blood bags. A part of them was going to become a part of someone else (and sometimes three people, when individual components are extracted). People have moments of insight when they realize they'll be helping to create up to three more "blood" relatives with every unit they offer. And they can do this several times a year!

So, if you know someone who's looking for more relatives, more meaning to their existence, or more joy in giving, you know what to tell them. You can go for it too. Like an oxygen mask in an airplane, you need to wear it first before assisting passengers next to you. Change starts with you (and me). When we change and lead by example, others will follow.

TIME FOR REFLECTION

- Have you ever participated in a blood donation camp?
- Would you be open to participating once? Or perhaps organizing a camp?

"Want to watch a miracle? Go and donate blood." - Unknown

World Blood Donor Day is observed on June 14th each year to raise awareness about the importance of blood donation and to thank blood donors for their life-saving contributions.

31

MOVING TO THE UNITED STATES

When Samyak was three, Anusha and I talked about moving to another country for a few years. It was the perfect time for us to relocate, since Anusha was on a career break and Samyak was three. The move didn't impact them. We wanted to experience living in another country. The flame of desire intensified as we discussed the benefits in several discussions. The flame soon transformed into a burning desire. I treated this like any other goal. I started exploring jobs in Dubai, Singapore, Australia, and the United States. After several weeks of research and initial job interviews in Dubai, I realized that moving to the United States would be the best option for us, given the weather and work culture. Plan A was international transfer through Oracle, Plan B was to find an employer that would facilitate this move. Plan C was moving to Dubai, Singapore, or Australia.

I discussed this with my manager Bence. He was supportive and said we need to make a strong case for this location transfer. I knew I had a good shot at this since I had a proven track record of strategic leadership and strong execution. Although we couldn't be certain about the outcome, we decided to give our best.

In support of my case, I took the lead on a new project in addition to my current role. This meant attending meetings during Indian nighttime two or three days a week. I acted as if I were already in the US time zone for meetings. It was like someone was testing the heat of our desire. We responded well as a family and managed to enjoy quality time together while taking on this additional responsibility.

The odds were 50-50 for our move—that was good enough. After four months, the odds increased, since my manager initiated the process formally, seeking corporate approval.

This was when our belief was bolstered. Anusha and I started planning and preparing for the move. We clearly laid out a plan for this. Our plan was written on a notepad. Every little detail was covered months before we actually boarded the flight.

The transfer request was approved in May 2015! In six months, our dream became a reality.

Working on legal documents was an arduous process, though it didn't appear that difficult considering our excitement for a new family life in another country.

We left India on October 7, 2015.

Some events in our lives happen through strong goals. This is one of those. It happened due to a burning desire, consistent work, follow-up, and a solid support system. I had multiple pathways to achieve this goal. If not for the US, we would have relocated to Dubai.

TIME FOR REFLECTION

- Do you want to move to another country to experience diversity?
- What options are you considering? Who can help you?

"When you know what you want and you want it bad enough, you'll find a way to get it." - Jim Rohn

32

FIREWALKING WITH TONY ROBBINS

One of the reasons for moving to the United States was attending workshops and conferences offered by some of my favorite authors and coaches. I wanted to attend Tony Robbins' seminar and experience walking on fire as part of his *Unleash the Power Within* three-day event. I had written this goal five years before this while reading Tony's book *Awaken the Giant Within*. His book had a deep impact on me. Several people had praised his live seminars and I wanted to attend one.

I put myself on the waitlist in 2015, right after moving to the US, for any upcoming seminar in the Bay Area. I was excited when it was happening in San Jose, an hour's drive from where I lived.

To get the best experience, I decided to stay in a hotel as opposed to commuting back and forth. The event was at the SAP Stadium in San Jose. I reached the venue to see a long line waiting to be checked in for the first evening's session. I was blown away as I entered the indoor stadium. More than 20,000 people were in that stadium for this seminar.

I had read Tony's books. His intensity and energy are at the top; you can feel it when you read his books or listen to his audio. What I like about him is his intensity to achieve his goals. He has built a billion-dollar business through his seminars and other related products and services—all through one person's vision. That's admirable and all entrepreneurs can learn a thing or two from this giant (both metaphorically and physically).

The first evening's primary attraction was walking on fire. For about three hours Tony talked about our state of mind and how it affects our behaviors. His laser-focused message that evening was, "Physiology drives psychology." He pumped up 20,000 people through physical movements and loud noises and tried to anchor that state of mind by yelling, "Yes, Yes, Yes," continuously.

After four hours, we went outside the stadium to walk on a bed of hot coals. Tony's team had set up at least 100 lanes paved with burning coals. Each lane was about four feet wide and 12 feet long. We could see hot coals being poured on those lanes every few minutes. People stood in line to walk through the fire screaming, "Yes." People walked on fire with bare feet. The scene was scary.

My heartbeat escalated and I wondered if I could really walk those 12 feet, which seemed like 12 miles for me at the time. Doubts swarmed my head as I waited for my turn. Fear, doubt, and uncertainty throttle us. That firewalk was a metaphor—a reminder of all sorts of fear in my life.

When my turn came, I walked slowly to ensure I bottled the feeling of accomplishing this long-cherished goal. As I walked, I realized the coal wasn't as hot as I imagined. It was uncomfortable, but not impossible, just like any other difficult goal in life.

I walked with fear in my mind and faith in myself. When I came to the end of the lane, I was ecstatic. I couldn't believe it was over. And I wanted *more*!

I went back for another trip. That sounds insane, but true. I stood in the line again for my second turn. During the second turn, I went slower to experience that moment fully and bottle it up for future recall. Taking all sensory imprints, I was able to anchor that experience in my mind and body.

The idea was to recall that experience whenever I felt fear paralyzing my actions throughout my life. This was a momentous achievement—a time to remember and I did everything to bottle it and soak every fiber of myself in that experience. I first heard about Tony's firewalk in 2011. I had waited five years to experience this event. I had moved to another country and got a chance to savor it. My goal had become a reality.

I was no longer controlled by fear. I become a person who can take action in spite of fear. Firewalk is a metaphor—a powerful one.

TIME FOR REFLECTION

- Do you want an experience to challenge your beliefs?
- What seminars or workshops can help you do it?

"Every problem is a gift—without problems we would not grow."
- Tony Robbins

Firewalking is found in many cultures around the world, including India, Fiji, Japan, Greece, Spain, and among Native American tribes. Each culture has its own rituals and beliefs associated with firewalking.

33

Waking up at 5:00 a.m. for 90 days of hot yoga

After moving to the United States, I ran a few races in the San Francisco Bay area. Training in the winter months was difficult. I wasn't used to running in colder temperatures. My energy withered like a leaf in the winter. I was looking for alternatives to keep myself fit during the coldest months in California. I came across a hot yoga class; also known as Bikram Yoga. I went for a trial class and immediately liked the series of postures. The only thing I didn't like was the excessive and artificially induced dry heat in the studio. The yoga poses were difficult too: Trikonasana, Utkatasana, Uthana Janu Shirshasana, etc.

This was a new adventure and I signed up for a 30-day challenge. That meant I would attend 30 classes in a row, without breaking the streak. There were three hurdles ahead of me on this journey.

1) Waking up at 5:00 a.m. 2) Staying in the hot studio for 90 minutes and 3) Learning to twist my body to meet the demands of those tough yoga poses.

I clubbed two goals here: waking up at five and keeping myself fit during winter months.

As usual, I set up a support system for my goals, starting with Anusha as an accountability partner. I took one day at a time and started showing up in the studio.

Wearing a T-shirt while practicing in a heated studio is a bad idea. T-shirts get soaked with sweat and later affect your movement and posture on the mat. I saw a couple of men doing poses without wearing a t-shirt; they just wore beach shorts. Inspired by them, I removed my t-shirt on the third day. It helped.

The studio had mirrored walls. We could see ourselves and our postures. Focusing on my postures helped me self-correct and maintain a high level of concentration by looking into my own eyes. I was not shy in removing my t-shirt, since I had lost 33 pounds (or 15 kilograms) of excess fat during my first two goals, between 2003 and 2005 (I hope you remember those goals). I was no longer uncomfortable seeing my body in a mirror. I didn't have thoughts of powerlessness or hopelessness.

I slowly picked up the 26 postures in Bikram Yoga. I loved the sequence of poses utilizing various parts of the body. The triangle pose, t-pose, eagle pose, and bow pose were really tough for me. They insisted on focus, concentration, and the ability to stretch my body beyond my natural capability.

I continued the streak by taking one day at a time. By the third week, I was able to get into most of the postures with relative ease, stay relaxed, and enjoy breathing. A couple of poses were still off the mark; they needed several months of consistent and mindful practice.

The head teacher appreciated my consistent effort in providing feedback and showing minor corrections. She noticed my flexibility and asked me to practice more for nurturing grace. It was a boost to my confidence.

A couple of other teachers also appreciated my focus, grace, and ability to learn difficult poses with patience and persistence. With all this heartfelt support, I continued the streak and completed the goal of a 30-day challenge. In fact, I continued the streak for *90* days.

After that, I strategically shifted and started integrating other forms of yoga. The studio offered many styles such as Iyengar yoga, Vinyasa flow, Gentle yin, and Family yoga. I tried all that for the next few months.

With this goal, I achieved several things. Most importantly, waking up at five in the morning, adjusting to the dry heat, learning difficult postures, and integrating several forms of Yoga into my training routine. Yoga is a great gift for runners to maintain flexibility, balance, and mindfulness.

TIME FOR REFLECTION

- Did you ever dream of joining the 5:00 a.m. club? What's stopping you?
- What benefits would you enjoy by waking up early? Are you ready to commit?

"Yoga allows you to find a new kind of freedom that you may not have known even existed." - B.K.S. Iyengar

In Hindu astrology and Vedic traditions, the Brahmi Muhurta is considered a highly auspicious time for performing spiritual, religious, or intellectual activities. Brahmi Muhurta is the last quarter of the night, typically occurring around *1.5 hours before sunrise.*

34

RUNNING A MARATHON: 42 BEFORE 40

I started running in 2009; my first race was a 10K. My first half marathon was in 2013. I ran 35 half marathons between 2013 and 2019, but wasn't ready to commit to a full marathon yet.

A full marathon requires more effort and time commitment for training. For long runs on weekends, you need three to four hours. Post-run recovery and self-care become critical too, so a lot of time is consumed for training and recovery. It affects family priorities and engagement.

In 2019, ten years after my first 10K, I decided to run a marathon. I was ready to commit to this goal. I had developed the habit of waking up at five in the morning by this time, so I could finish all my workouts by eight (three-hour runs on Sundays, 90-minute runs on Tuesdays and Thursdays).

Anusha was fully supportive. I wanted to run a 42-kilometer race before turning 40! So *42 before 40* became a burning desire in 2019.

I chose a race in San Diego for this goal. There were seven months to train and build my capacity. Doubling the distance from 21 (half marathon) to 42 kilometers (full marathon) is daunting: mentally and physically.

I ramped up the distance slowly, working with a professional running coach, Ash Nath. Ash is a thirteen-time qualifier for the Boston Marathon, an iconic race commonly termed the "Olympics for amateur runners."

I added Epsom salt and ice baths on Sundays for added recovery after long runs.

Inspired by Brendan Brazier, Canadian athlete and author, I turned vegan in 2019. I was fully on a plant-based diet while training for marathons that year.

While training for this race, I developed a solid mental toughness and resilience. Because of the added distance, I had additional strength training during this time. That's why I love working with an experienced coach like Ash. He knew my weak links and the training plan was crafted to address them.

My goal was to finish the marathon in four hours and twelve minutes or under, at the pace of 10 kilometers per hour. And I didn't want to take any break during the race as walking was not acceptable to me in a race. The entire training plan was focused on this goal.

We traveled to San Diego as a family for this race. The family planned to stay a couple of days after the race to explore sunny San Diego.

There were more than 10,000 runners on the race day. It was a huge crowd. The adrenaline of runners was in the air. I could feel it in every breath.

I followed the racing plan up to 35 kilometers. At the 35-kilometer mark, I took a minute break to stretch my calves. I continued slowly because I didn't want to walk during the race. My goal was to run the whole distance and I was determined to do it.

As I crossed the 40-kilometer mark, I was excited, knowing I had only two more to go. I increased the pace for the last two kilometers. I crossed the finish line in four hours and four minutes—8 minutes faster than my original goal. Moreover, I didn't walk any time during the race; I *ran* the whole marathon distance.

The moment I crossed the finish line, I could call myself a *marathoner*. It was a euphoric moment—a moment of realization that our limits are not real; the limits are in the mind and I can transcend them.

TIME FOR REFLECTION

- When have you truly given your best, your all, to something?
- What do you think the outcomes would be if you did so more frequently?

"Confidence is not some nonphysical quality snatched from the spiritual dimension and installed in the mind. It is the feeling that arises when the body's knowledge of itself is in harmony with a person's dreams." - Matt Fitzgerald

The term *marathon* traces back to ancient Greece, specifically the town of Marathon, named after the plant "marathos" (fennel). Legend links it to Pheidippides' run from Marathon to Athens in 490 BCE to announce victory over Persia, covering approximately 26 miles. The modern marathon race emerged from this narrative, established as an event in the inaugural 1896 Olympic Games in Athens. The distance of 26.2 miles (or 42 kilometers) was standardized in the twentieth century.

35

RUNNING A MARATHON IN UNDER FOUR HOURS

After completing my first marathon, I was eager to set my sights on the next milestone as a runner. I wanted to attempt a sub-4 marathon. Based on my training volume that year and performance in San Diego, my coach, Ash Nath was fully supportive. We had four months until the next race. I began training in the third week of July.

Applying the lessons from the San Diego race, I trained well for the second marathon. I did back-to-back runs on three weekends three weeks before the race day, running 15 miles on Saturday and Sunday. Also, there was more emphasis on strength training in this training plan. Additional strength would help me sustain the pace in the last five kilometers.

We traveled as a family to Las Vegas for this race. To get the best experience of the event, we stayed at the Venetian Hotel. It was right across from the finish line of the race. The logistics were super convenient for this race. The start line was a 15-minute walk from the hotel; the finish line was right across from it.

It was an evening race, starting at 5:00 p.m. The temperature was warm. Walking around the Vegas Strip in the evening helped me understand the reasons behind the race time. It's cooler in the evening, too warm before that.

I did a meticulous job in following the plan until the 39-kilometer mark. Based on my watch, it appeared I would finish the race in just above four hours. I didn't want to miss this goal. I wanted to achieve the goal at any cost.

I knew Samyak and Anusha would be waiting at the finish line. They were eager to see me finish and achieve my goal in this race. I decided to pick up the pace and cover the remaining two kilometers faster. My goal was to sprint the last 500 meters.

I did as planned. I saw the finish line and glowing lights near the Vegas strip, right across from the famous Venetian hotel. I started sprinting. I gave it everything I had. There was a lot at stake—months of training, years of waiting to do a sub-4 marathon, and decades of work on my fitness and athletic ability.

Samyak and Anusha saw me in the last stretch. They were yelling and cheering to get my attention. I was lost in my goal to save every second I could, to leave no stone unturned to achieve my goal. I crossed the finish line. Looking at my watch, I sighed. It was three hours and 59 minutes. I had achieved my goal! I finished a marathon in under four hours.

More than me, Anusha and Samyak were relieved that the goal was off my back. Perhaps they were worried I would sign up for another marathon to achieve my timing goal.

Samyak was a bit surprised that I didn't hear their cheer or respond to them. I explained to him about the "zone" and how we get absorbed and get into ultra-focus mode. We had a great time as a family after the race eating at restaurants and walking around downtown Las Vegas.

I turned 40 in September 2019, ran a 42K race in June 2019 before I turned 40, and then I achieved a sub-4 marathon goal in November 2019. I *reshaped* my identity that year. I grew younger. My fitness level, resilience, and confidence reached a whole new level. This gave a solid foundation for me to tackle several challenges in personal and professional domains.

TIME FOR REFLECTION

- What is your ideal fitness level?
- What actions can you take this year to achieve that level of physical fitness?

"Like the marathon, life can sometimes be difficult, challenging and present obstacles, however if you believe in your dreams and never ever give up, things will turn out for the best." - Meb Keflezighi

Running a marathon in under four hours requires maintaining an average pace of approximately nine minutes and nine seconds per mile (or five minutes and 41 seconds per kilometer), which is considered a challenging but achievable pace for many experienced runners.

36

ATTAINING THE TOUGHEST COACH CERTIFICATION

I n 2013, I bumped into *Philosopher's Notes* by Brian Johnson. Brian had read hundreds of non-fiction books and created the summary of each book into a six-page document. He creatively named them *Philosopher's Notes*. I became a subscriber of his service; those notes were great. By 2019, he had thousands of subscribers loving his notes and other curated materials he sold on his website.

Brian launched a coach certification program in January 2019. I attended a webinar to understand what the program entailed. Unlike other programs, this was totally focused on personal transformation through daily habits and routines. The program was an intersection of ancient wisdom and modern science. The program is called Heroic Coach Certification.

I had several certificates in coaching under my belt already, but all of them focused on helping me bring out the best in a *client*—and my expertise as a coach. The focus was more on the client's transformation, not on my own hero's journey.

The Heroic program is totally different. In my experience, it's the toughest certification program, because it challenges coaches to *practice* what they preach. One example to illustrate: the coaches are expected to maintain a healthy waist-to-hip ratio. I loved it! We need to be in good shape to feel energetic and to show up as the best version of ourselves.

There's no other coaching certification that holds coaches to high standards of optimal living. In my view, a coach's lifestyle matters. They need to be radiant examples of the virtues they want to see in their clients. That's why this goal attracted me, even though it wasn't an easy one.

Heroic was all about my *own* transformation: personal vision and consistent action.

This was a 300-day program with a weekly online meeting with Brian and all other participants.

The program also had several prolific authors as guest faculties to share wisdom and offer coaching tools. Through this program, I was able to learn from 600 plus books and 50 plus luminary authors.

I loved the book summaries, self-paced classes, and live sessions on mental fitness, sports psychology, and stoicism; they are my all-time favorites. Through this program, I was able to attend live Q&A sessions with mental performance coaches who have worked with sports celebrities like Michael Jordan, LeBron James, and many Olympic athletes.

As a coach, I also loved group coaching sessions twice a week where Brian coached participants on topics of their concern. Watching such conversations honed my coaching skills.

I developed several productive lifestyle habits and routines in this 300-day journey: walking 10,000 steps every day, eating dinner before seven at night, sleeping early, 12-hour digital fasting, journaling, and designing my own morning rituals.

I fell in love with journaling in the morning. My all-time favorite journaling question is *"How can I get paid for doing what I love?"*

I might have answered this question in writing more than a hundred times. And I did get the answer: *Learn, grow, and serve people through my knowledge and example.*

By September 2019, I had finished all the requirements for this coach certification. I looked forward to the graduation ceremony on December 8th. As usual, we made this a family affair, since family support was pivotal during the 300-day journey. Anusha and Samyak joined me for the graduation day.

Twenty-nineteen was a year of transformation through the Heroic Coach program. It was a lifestyle reset. I brought changes in my approach to fitness, eating habits, and sleeping patterns. I became a better person, a loving husband, an exemplary father, and a fearless coach who practices instead of preaching. I'm a lifetime Heroic coach who is committed to following this path for years to come.

It's always the case that the process of achieving goals transforms us. The journey is the destination!

TIME FOR REFLECTION

- What's working well for you in three areas: eating habits, physical fitness, and sleep quality?
- What tiny changes can you make in your choices today to optimize them?

"Heroic is the best self-development platform in the world." - John Mackey, co-founder and former CEO of Whole Foods Market

Heroic program is used by world-class coaches and trainers including the Miami Heat's Coach Spo (*the* highest paid coach in North American sports history), NCAA Championship-winning coach Brian O'Connor, and founding director of the Master of Applied Positive Psychology (MAPP) program at the University of Pennsylvania, Dr. James Pawelski.

37

RUNNING A SPARTAN RACE

Heroic Coach Certification aspirants were required to demonstrate their physical fitness through a racing event (or equivalent activity) or run a Spartan race (3 miles / 5 kilometers) that was part of the graduation weekend in Los Angeles in December 2019.

Technically, I had ticked all the boxes by September. Since I was already running marathons, I didn't need to sign for a Spartan race. In fact, I didn't even know what a Spartan race was.

I read about the history of Spartan races and the kinds of obstacles in the race. I was intrigued. I had run marathons, but I realized the obstacle course race demanded strength and resilience. I had enough reasons to work on this goal. I started preparing for a three-mile race, called a *sprint*, which includes 13 obstacles along the course.

This race required me to go through a lot of discomfort such as wading through a lake, walking in muddy water, crawling under barbed wires, and a few other obstacles that were placed across the route. You can check the internet for various kinds of obstacles in this race. They're creative, demanding, and need physical strength, an acid test for your mental resilience too.

I knew I wouldn't be able to cross all 13 obstacles since it needed months of training to do that. For each obstacle you don't cross, you need to do 10 burpees as a penalty in a Spartan race.

So I did a lot of burpees from September to December to strengthen myself. Trust me, it's not easy to do 10 burpees *in the middle of a race* when your body is smeared with mud and dust and you're running three miles!

The race was in Los Angeles, a day before the graduation ceremony of this Heroic certification. Samyak and Anusha watched me run this race in a large open park. It was so much fun.

With all the upfront training, I crossed nine obstacles successfully. For the remaining four, I did 40 burpees, 10 for each missed obstacle. Every obstacle was a reminder: *Obstacles are the way, and the only way out is through!*

This graduation event on December 8, 2019, was more exciting than anything else I have witnessed in my entire life in academics. I'm not exaggerating, it's 100 percent true.

I have the Heroic graduation certificate on the wall next to my desk. It's one of the greatest achievements of my life.

The obstacle race is yet another metaphor for challenges in life. We move through them, they make us stronger, and bring the best version alive. They show us what we are made of.

TIME FOR REFLECTION

• Are you facing any obstacles in your life right now?
• What will change if you adopt the mindset "The obstacle is the way"?

"Your main obstacle is you. You are also your greatest opportunity."
- Joe De Sena

The ancient Spartans were known for their unique way of life, which emphasized discipline, military prowess, and simplicity. The term *Spartan* has come to be associated with qualities such as austerity, self-discipline, and resilience, reflecting the values and lifestyle of the ancient Spartan society.

38

SINGING KARAOKE

In 2017, I was in Bengaluru for a business visit. The team had organized a karaoke night followed by dinner. I had never experienced karaoke before. As we waited our turn, I heard other people sing with passion and grace. They were totally immersed in singing and synching with the background music while reading lyrics on a large display screen. It was fun listening and watching people express themselves freely. Karaoke is an act of self-expression.

The shadow of self-consciousness and timidity disappears with a mic in hand. It was our turn. I wanted to sing but I didn't know any songs at the time. The real fun is in singing songs that you like, that you have heard several times, and I had none. So, I took this as a goal.

A month later, we purchased a karaoke set. It had a powerful speaker, mic, and disco lights. It was a perfect set. Almost every weekend, during the evenings, I would try one or two songs. I listened to some of my favorite songs over and over to understand the rhythm, beats, and lyrics. I learned songs from three languages: English, Hindi, and Kannada.

After a few weeks, I became good at it. I love low-pitched, slow, and melodious songs. My mood elevates when I sing. All thoughts slow down. I'm in the flow. I was hooked on this. It's a great stress buster. I thoroughly enjoyed the process.

Over the next six months, I learned to sing over a hundred songs. My original goal was 25 songs—I passed it *fourfold*. I also had an opportunity to sing a couple of songs at a family gathering with 50 people in the room.

This has become a family ritual now. I sing once every week. I do it with friends and family and really enjoy it. In addition to the flow state, it's a fine form of self-expression, silencing the inner voice of judgment. The act is a stop sign for timidity and shyness.

Anusha and I sing some songs together. She loves it too. I also love jamming with Samyak. He does a good job as well and he sings some of his favorites. I'm glad he doesn't feel shy. Shyness acts as a speedbreaker; it slows down one's enthusiasm for life.

Even though I had overcome shyness with repeated speeches in Toastmasters, I experienced it anew when I began singing karaoke. Awareness is like sunlight. It cuts through the fog of doubt, insecurity, and confusion.

Once you know what's blocking you, you can do something about it. Take action. Grow. Improve. Express fully. Live life with full intention. Go *beyond your limits*.

TIME FOR REFLECTION

- In what situations do you find yourself holding back?
- What would change if you could express yourself fully?

"He who sings scares away his woes." - Miguel de Cervantes

The term *karaoke* has its origins in Japan and is a combination of two Japanese words: *kara*, meaning "empty," and *okesutora*, which is a loanword from English meaning "orchestra." Together, *karaoke* translates to "empty orchestra."

39

SOLVING 600 CODING PROBLEMS

To prepare for technical interviews in big technology companies, I set a goal to solve 100 coding problems in 2020. However, I ended up solving over 600 problems on Leetcode in 12 months while working as director of a technology organization at Oracle.

You wonder why? I'll tell you.

One day while journaling in January 2020, I reflected on my career: eighteen years in the industry, all with one organization. Oracle—thirteen years in India and five in the United States. I didn't like the narrative; it needed some spice. Something was missing. I asked, "When would I feel content about my career? When would I feel like there's nothing left for me in a software-related job?"

Questions are powerful; quality questions evoke quality answers. I had the answer right in front of me, scribbled in my journal. The answer was *FAANG*. It's a popular acronym for five big technology companies, Facebook, Apple, Amazon, Netflix, and Google—the five most popular and respected tech companies in the world.

I wanted to work at one of these companies for a few years before embarking on my coaching business. Clarity is a superpower! My plan was to work in a FAANG company for 5–8 years and then *by age 50 start a coaching company.* I had a clear 10-year personal vision—a compelling vision as a compass.

FAANG interviews are well-structured. They assess managers' technical skills. I had heard that a coding test would be involved. I had closed the door on coding in 2010. After that, all my focus was on building organizations, delivering results, and growing people. So, I needed to refresh my coding skills to ensure this gap wouldn't *narrow* my options for interviews.

I went on to a popular coding platform: Leetcode. Within a month, I solved 100 easy-level coding problems. I enjoyed the process since they were simple problems. After that, I hit a snag with medium and hard problems. I couldn't make further progress because I had forgotten the various algorithms and data structures needed for solving the problems.

I could have stopped at 100 problems. However, I wanted to ensure I revisited the fundamentals of data structures and algorithms before managing engineering teams in FANNG companies. My goal was now to solve 600 algorithmic problems that cover common real-world problems in the industry and SQL problems that cover data engineering challenges. Through my effort and achievement, I wanted to give hope to other people who dread these technical interviews. Especially experienced engineers and managers.

I carved out 60 minutes each day. I read books, took online courses, and did a few one-on-one sessions with senior engineers and technical leads in my network. Some engineers at Oracle were helpful too. We solved problems together and discussed various approaches. It was a great opportunity to build connections. People were surprised by my interest in solving these coding puzzles and appreciated the growth mindset I demonstrated.

In this process, I became more empathetic to engineers who go through these interviews and then design algorithms to solve complex real-life challenges to serve millions of users.

With this feat accomplished, I was ready for any technical interview that would test my problem-solving and algorithmic thinking. In fact, I looked forward to it and there was no trace of fear in my mind. I said goodbye to Leetcode after solving *648* problems.

TIME FOR REFLECTION

- Do you think your age is a barrier to any of your goals?
- What if you adopted the mindset that "age is just a number"? How would that change things?

It's not what we do once in a while that shapes our lives. It's what we do consistently." - Tony Robbins

40

MASTERING STORYTELLING FOR JOB INTERVIEWS

While I ramped up my coding skills and solved coding problems, technical recruiters from various tech companies approached me. I spoke to them to understand the interview details. I learned about another aspect of leadership interviews: behavioral interview questions.

Since I had not interviewed for eighteen long years; this was a critical skill to master. The most common question for me would be, "Why are you looking for a job after eighteen years at Oracle?" This question needs a thoughtful answer, a compelling narrative. Hence it became a goal to pursue and achieve mastery in storytelling.

Behavioral interviews entail two types of questions. One focuses on a candidate's past experience in handling a specific management or leadership scenario. The other attempts to understand their mental model or approach to handling challenging situations with people or projects.

The premise of this type of interview is this: your past behaviors and successes are indicators of how well you'll handle a similar situation in the future. There's some truth to this, although over-indexing on a perfect answer may reject qualified candidates just because they don't give well-rounded answers to these questions.

As a candidate, you need to do your homework and pick the right stories in these interviews. That's your responsibility. There's no point in blaming the interview process. The company is doing their best to recruit people who can help them achieve their business goals. Your job is to demonstrate you can help them accomplish their goal.

I had learned about the *hero's journey* coined by Dr. Joseph Campbell during a coach training program in 2014. I reread his book *The Hero with a Thousand Faces* to leverage his framework for interview questions. It's a wonderful framework for storytelling. This became my go-to framework for telling career stories in two to three minutes for behavioral questions.

I listed common questions asked in leadership interviews and started answering them in a story format using the hero's journey framework. The Hero's journey framework was also helpful in developing a compelling narrative on my LinkedIn profile and resume.

Initially, I resisted this type of interview. I didn't like being graded or measured by the quality of my answers. However, in a few weeks, I started enjoying this exercise. It invited me to reflect on an eighteen-year career and collect leadership stories and my personal frameworks for handling situations at work.

I had wonderful leadership stories from my experience of working in India and the United States. I thought they were not good enough until I realized "not good enough" was a story I was making up in my mind. It wasn't real. This was a real breakthrough as I prepared stories for interviews.

With all this preparation. I was fully equipped to face both types of interviews: technical and behavioral.

I started applying for jobs on LinkedIn. I interviewed at a few low-stakes companies for practice before appearing for interviews at FAANG companies. Mastering the art of storytelling was helpful, and I did well in these test interviews. I didn't accept any offer from those companies, but the experience bolstered my confidence as a candidate. An offer letter is a potent antidote to imposter syndrome.

TIME FOR REFLECTION

- What stories do you tell about yourself?
- How can you start telling empowering stories more often?

"The cave you fear to enter holds the treasure you seek." - Dr. Joseph Campbell

The Hero with a Thousand Faces by Joseph Campbell explores the concept of the monomyth, or hero's journey, found in myths worldwide. Campbell outlines the archetypal journey of the hero, from the ordinary world to adventure, trials, and transformation, culminating in a return with newfound wisdom. He identifies common stages in this journey, including the Call to Adventure, Meeting the Mentor, and the Ordeal. Through comparative mythology, Campbell demonstrates the universal themes and symbols that shape human stories, revealing a shared quest for meaning and self-realization. His work has influenced literature, film, psychology, and spiritual philosophy, offering insights into the human condition.

41

RECEIVING THE JOB OFFER
FROM META

Once I developed confidence by interviewing at smaller companies, I went back to the recruiters at Facebook and Google. Building a great rapport with recruiters helps. The recruiter at Google scheduled the interviews.

A month later, I had an interview at Google, actually five interviews spread over two days. I did well. Their next step was team-matching interviews. It was an attempt to place candidates in the best team possible based on their backgrounds.

While I was waiting for that to happen, a recruiter from Facebook reached out. The role seemed interesting—more than the role, it was the *goal* that pulled me. I was ready for any of these FAANG companies. That's the power of clarity—the *why* has to be clear.

This was a data engineering manager role and required me to solve SQL and Python coding problems in the technical interview. The first interview was a 45-minute technical screening. I did an excellent job. The interviewer's response was a clear indicator. We finished the interview in 30 minutes and I solved all the problems. Armed with solid preparation, not only did I solve the problems, but I also articulated my solutions with confidence.

The recruiter shared feedback on my performance, openly sharing positive feedback signals from the interviewer. I then had five rounds of interviews spread over two days.

The last interview was fun. It was with a VP of Data Engineering. I went with a well-manicured slide deck. He laughed and said, "You're overprepared. I haven't seen anyone come to a technical vision interview with a slide deck. You'll get bonus points for this effort."

A week later, the recruiter called for an offer discussion. I asked for an initial offer from their side by giving them a broad range. I had heard of insane salary ranges at Facebook and I quoted a broad range that would help me negotiate better.

Their initial offer was decent. But I asked for more since I deserved it. Most importantly, I *had* demonstrated my value during the interview process. I created leverage through my performance and my track record.

The experience of negotiating was a moment of personal growth. It was another reminder that what we become through goals is as important as the achievement—sometimes more important.

Two days later, I received a call from the recruiter. He stated the numbers: base, bonus, and stock options. A minute later the offer letter popped into my inbox. I was blown away. I accepted the offer *immediately*!

I ran out of my room and started screaming, jumping, and punching in the air. Twelve months of disciplined effort had come to fruition. Samyak and Anusha were elated to see me jumping around the house like an athlete who had won a gold medal in the Olympics. They had seen me work on this goal for twelve months, a minimum of 60 minutes every day, all seven days per week!

There's power in consistent effort. It compounds. We may not see it in a few days or weeks. Wait for a few months to be surprised by the changes you'll see.

This phenomenon applies to everything in life: health, wealth, business, and many more. Consistency is greater than intensity. With consistency, you build habits of thinking and behaving. They become natural to you. Chores become effortless, boring becomes flowing, and difficult becomes easy.

After a few weeks' break, I joined Meta on December 6, 2021. Facebook became Meta a week after I accepted the offer, so the acronym changed to *MAANG* from *FAANG,* but my offer letter still has Facebook on it.

With this goal achieved, I was one step closer to my 10-year vision—to become a coach and start my own coaching company after a stint at Meta.

TIME FOR REFLECTION

- What's your dream job?
- Which employer do you admire, and what are the key elements of your admiration?

"I accumulated small but consistent habits that ultimately led to results that were unimaginable when I started." - James Clear

The term *meta* comes from ancient Greek, where it originally meant "beyond or after." In Greek, *meta* is a preposition that indicates a change or transition, often implying movement from one state to another. Over time, *meta* has been adopted into various languages, including English, where it is used as a prefix to denote concepts that are self-referential, abstract, or transcendent.

42

BECOMING A BETTER WRITER

As an organizational leader, my role at Meta required a lot of writing. This was a new skill for me. I was great at writing long-form speeches (from Toastmasters experience), but that style of writing would not work in writing business messages that are short, crisp, and to the point.

Enter a new goal: *Becoming a better writer.*

I bought a couple of books and started reading them immediately. There were a few leaders whom I admired at Meta, especially their writing skills. I sought mentorship with two other senior leaders. Finding mentors is a surefire way to improve and deal with imposter thoughts.

At Meta, all written communication happens on a tool called Workplace. This is a Facebook-like social platform for business entities. Anything you post there is seen by thousands of employees. Someone who is not actively writing on social media would naturally feel uncomfortable posting on this type of platform.

I started writing small bits of content to get feedback from others. The first post I made on organizational vision was daunting. It took three weeks to write a post of 600 words.

With all the other smart people at Meta writing well-structured content, it felt odd to be writing something unworthy, although the word "unworthy" was a random thought in my mind with no evidence to back up the argument. That's how impostor syndrome starts, through *thoughts*! We then water this plant with more and more thoughts, nurturing it until it grows into a tree.

I pushed through the inertia and imposter feeling, modifying my document several times. Finally, I posted it in several Workplace groups. Some of these groups had several thousand employees.

My first post was about three months after I joined the company. I put a ton of effort into polishing my writing skills at that time. I had a lot to make up for.

If you remember my story, you know I started learning the English language at age 11 and English is my third language. I had covered the foundational gap in Toastmasters' journey, but this was a level higher in stakes. Brevity, clarity, and simplicity in writing were skills worth mastering.

Every job has opportunities to gather skills that help in our lives. We need to ensure we give 100 percent to what we do to master the skills. I'm glad I grabbed this opportunity to sharpen my writing during my tenure at Meta. I wrote one post every week during my stint there. I wrote "1PAW" on a sticky note to remind me about writing *"1 Post A Week."*

Today, as a solopreneur, when I write on LinkedIn or create presentations, people appreciate the brevity and clarity in my writing, thanks to my Meta experience. It was a rite of passage for quality writing—a crucible for removing dross in business writing. It was an experience to remember and a life-long lesson and skill that's invaluable—these are gifts from my tenure at Meta.

TIME FOR REFLECTION

- On a scale of 1 to 10, how would you rate your writing skills?
- What can you do this year to improve your writing skills?

"The secret to good writing is rewriting." - William Zinsser

Writing activates the prefrontal cortex, involved in planning, decision-making, and problem-solving. It requires organization of thoughts, holding information in working memory, and inhibiting distractions. The prefrontal cortex regulates attention, monitors goals, and aids in problem-solving during writing. Language production, including word retrieval and grammar processing, also engages the prefrontal cortex. Regular writing practice strengthens cognitive functions associated with the prefrontal cortex, leading to improved writing skills and executive function.

43

RUNNING A 10K RACE IN 46 MINUTES

After running two full marathons in 2019, I turned my focus toward half marathons to balance my time across other areas of life. I improved my half marathon speed during this time with my best time at one hour and 40 minutes.

I attempted a half marathon in 2021 with the goal of beating my best time. I didn't make it. Right after the race, I went to the on-site registration counter and I registered for next year's race in 2022. I didn't anticipate my professional goals coming in the way when I signed up for the race. I didn't know I would be working at Meta while I registered.

Within weeks of joining Meta, I realized that training for a half marathon was unrealistic. There was so much to learn and do as part of onboarding into a new job. Loading all the necessary business and product context is critical for success at impact-oriented companies like Meta. This is especially true for leadership roles.

After discussing this with my coach, I picked a new goal that would help me stay fit while being fully engaged in a new job that was demanding. A goal is a compass setting the direction of life.

Since 2017, San Jose Rock 'n' Roll has been my favorite race. I run this every year in October. I decided to improve my 10K race timing in 2022. With 10K races, the workouts are short and quick. Since the workouts are shorter, the recovery will be faster too. This was a comeback strategy for better performance later; it was a deliberate detour from half marathons to 10K races to become a better runner and because it fit my work priorities better.

My goal was to finish the 10K in less than 46 minutes. My personal best was 48 minutes before this event. I wanted to stretch and achieve this goal as a new challenge (since I moved away from the goal of a half marathon in less than one hour 40 minutes). Shaving off two minutes was a compromise for missing the half-marathon goal.

I trained for three months: July, August, and September. My mother came to see me run this race along with Anusha and Samyak. This was my first 10K race after a long time. For several years, I had run half marathon races in this same event.

I did well and finished the race in 46 minutes. By focusing on a shorter race, I achieved a new personal best timing and, in the process, my fitness improved considerably.

The icing on the cake: I came in *third* in my age category. For the first time, I was among the top finishers in a race. This was huge for me!

My mother was super proud of this feat. I am so glad she witnessed my performance. She has seen my sustained transformation over *twenty* years; she appreciates my goal-oriented lifestyle. Since "words of affirmation" is not her love language she doesn't express her feelings in words. But the joy in her welled-up eyes, the warm hug, and the pat on my back after the race expressed her true feelings of love and pride. They were more precious than the race medal.

What seemed a setback earlier, decreasing the distance to 10 kilometers, was a blessing in disguise. I learned a lesson about being flexible in goal achievement, embracing the constraints of reality, and adjusting my goals accordingly while remaining on the original path.

There was a blessing in this lesson and a lesson in the blessing.

TIME FOR REFLECTION

- Are you currently struggling to make progress on a challenging goal?
- How can you scale back or minify this goal? Could there be any lessons in this situation?

"When defeat comes, accept it as a signal that your plans are not sound, rebuild those plans, and set sail once more toward your coveted goal." - Napoleon Hill

44

STARTING A COACHING COMPANY

I n 2021, after 19 years at Oracle, I joined Meta as an organizational leader. This was a milestone in my 10-year vision of ultimately starting a coaching company at age 50. It was a strategic move. There was a solid reason to join Meta. I enjoyed the glory, monetary benefits, and oomph of being employed at a coveted company like Meta.

The work at Meta was challenging. It stretched my abilities as a leader, coach, and communicator. The experience propelled me to learn new skills and become a more mindful, strategic, and authentic leader.

As an employee, it was an exceptional opportunity to listen to Mark Zuckerberg and his executive leadership team in weekly Q&A sessions. I attended every one of them during my tenure. For managers who are hungry to learn and grow, these weekly live sessions are micro classes in strategic thinking and executive communication.

Changes in the economy and massive job cuts impacted many companies in 2022 and 2023. My position at Meta was eliminated. This was a surprise for me and the 11,000 people that were impacted. Here's the rub, this layoff was not based on performance.

I felt like someone pulled the rug out from under me. I was totally unprepared and had no clue about my next move.

However, this event didn't upset me or make me feel like a victim. To me, this was an opportunity to apply all the mental toughness and resilience I gathered since 2003, putting principles into practice. I was my first coaching client! It was a time for leading by example, showing what I was made of.

I took a 90-day break to reflect and decide the next steps. During this break, I explored a few job openings to determine if I wanted to pursue those roles. I spoke to a couple of recruiters and hiring managers at a few tech companies. I didn't find the roles appealing.

I had worked for 21 years in the tech industry—a half marathon in years. I wasn't keen to run a full marathon (42 kilometers). I wanted to do something more impactful. I wanted to follow my passion and put my career capital to good use. Being in middle management was too narrow compared to the breadth of my personal vision.

I knew what I would do if money weren't a constraint: *Coaching, training, and mentoring.* The answer was in my face. I already had a 10-year personal vision, doing this at age 50. I did this in India as a freelance consultant and proved that I could earn income doing it.

The question was: can this profession provide a sustainable income in the US? I didn't know. I also knew I wouldn't know if I didn't try.

With lots of deliberation over two months, I crafted a two-year plan with many milestones to set up a coaching business. Even if this didn't replace my job income, I knew I could set up a side income in two years. After that, I could decide to pursue this full-time or part-time with additional employment.

Either way, this was a win for me, full-time or part-time. Additionally, I had two full years to run all sorts of experiments in this domain. Do, learn, make mistakes, and repeat!

So I plunged in. On February 28th, 2023, I registered a single-member LLC *Changesmith Coaching* in California focused on coaching and training, fulfilling my long-term goal of being a leadership coach and facilitator.

I coined the word *Changesmith* on the lines of goldsmith, blacksmith, and wordsmith. *Changesmith* is a person who is skilled at *conscious behavioral changes.* It encapsulates my coaching philosophy and my evolution. A changesmith is skilled in changing thoughts and behaviors!

I could have returned to the known world of employment in a technology organization. That's what I did for 21 years, so going back was an easy choice—the path of least resistance. A choice that didn't have mojo, personal growth, and a sense of satisfaction.

Without the job cut at Meta, I would have waited another *five to eight years* to start my own coaching company. My original plan was to do it at age 50, and with this "fortunate" event I started at 43.

In a way I'm grateful to Meta and the slow economy for pushing me to achieve this goal sooner than later saving seven precious years of my life.

TIME FOR REFLECTION

- If you were to start your company, what product or service would you offer?
- Could you take a bold step and register your company as a business entity? You don't have to stop what you're doing. Simply register a business after talking to your accountant. You'll feel empowered.

"Circumstances don't make the man; they only reveal him to himself." - Epictetus

The term *entrepreneur* has its roots in French. It derives from the Old French word *entreprendre*, which means "to undertake or to take in hand." The word itself is a combination of *entre*, meaning "between," and *prendre*, meaning "to take."

45

SIGNING UP COACHING CLIENTS

Right after starting *Changesmith Coaching*, I was determined to achieve a specific revenue goal in 2023. That was my first milestone in the two-year business plan. I had nine months to achieve the goal; and a series of experiments to run for collecting data.

Goal setting is a mindset for me, a way of approaching life situations. I wrote the goal on an index card so I could see it frequently.

Samyak made a lovely digital art on his iPad, crafting an image that became a wallpaper on my phone. Touching my phone was a reminder to take action toward my goal. I touch my phone sparingly. Even then it was a creative way to remind myself to stay on the path. When I derailed, l could trace back and walk on the path again.

My first goal was to sign up a few clients for one-on-one coaching engagements. These are three to six-month engagements, and the payment is made up front.

One-on-one coaching was easy to start. I earned several certifications over the years and have more than 10 years of practical experience in coaching. The biggest challenge was finding clients!

As an organizational leader, this was never a problem. I always had people coming to me for coaching. In my career, I have coached several people that were outside my organization.

Whenever someone knew about my background and my association with Toastmasters and visited my website, they would explore if I could coach them. I always said *yes* with excitement, even though these were pro bono engagements.

Coaching conversations brought excitement to me, helping others raise awareness through meaningful and reflective conversations.

The coachee's mind is like a Rubik's cube. Through a conversation, a jumbled mind can rearrange itself into a neatly arranged cube. Since I have worked with coaches as a client, I have experienced this. It is not just a 'woo-woo' feeling; it is a felt experience. Clarity is the primary reason people love coaching conversations. An uncluttered mind is powerful.

The more we openly talk about challenges and our approaches to surmounting them, the better we feel and act in the pursuit of resolving them. Creating this awareness is where a coach comes in handy. They help you see what you don't want to or can't see. A coach holds a mirror for you to see yourself, seeing reality *as it is* with no distortion.

There are many books on coaching frameworks and tools. Books on finding clients? Not many exist and they are rare to find, especially for new coaches who are looking for potential clients.

Luckily, I bumped into Steve Chandler's books on this subject. I applied the strategies from the books right away. An ounce of action is better than pounds of information. I offered complimentary sessions to thirty people I knew who would benefit from a coaching engagement.

I found three paying clients within 30 days. *WOW!* I was a paid coach. The posture of your pitch is different when you have paying clients. In 90 days, I signed up 10 clients. I enjoyed working with these people every week, helping them make steady progress on their cherished goals. Some signed up for three months and some for six months.

The biggest learning from this experience: offer complimentary coaching sessions to help people experience the benefits. People don't know what coaching can do for them. Experiences cannot be expressed in words. Coaching falls into this experience 100 percent.

Here's the exciting part: my hourly coaching rate is more than the hourly salary at Meta (based on the base salary). Of course, we cannot include bonuses and equity in this calculation, but it showed my value in the marketplace. I knew I was onto something exciting.

Armed with this self-confidence, cash flow, and paying clients, I was ready for my next challenge. I had solved the leadership development problem for an audience, now it was time to scale.

TIME FOR REFLECTION

- Have you ever worked with a coach?
- What if you treat yourself as an athlete in the arena of life? How can a coach help you?

"Everybody Needs a Coach. Everyone." - Dr. Atul Gawande

The term *coaching* originates from the Hungarian village of Kocs, where horse-drawn carriages, known as "coaches," were first produced. Over time, the term came to describe the individuals who guided these carriages. In the 19th century, it evolved metaphorically to denote those who provided guidance and instruction. Today, coaching spans various fields, including sports, business, and personal development, where coaches support individuals in achieving goals, overcoming obstacles, and realizing their potential.

46

RUNNING A **10K** RACE IN UNDER **45** MINUTES

O ne of the holy grails of a runner is to run a 10K race in under 45 minutes. All seasoned runners aim to achieve this timing goal. I admired runners who could accomplish this. You enter a different league when you can do this. It requires great fitness and aerobic capacity.

I have seen several lean runners do this, but deep down I didn't believe it was for me. But now that I had 46 minutes under my belt, shaving off another minute didn't seem impossible. Going from 75 to 45 minutes is a "snap" goal whereas 46 to under 45 minutes is a "stretch" goal. So I went for this goal.

This 10K race was part of the annual San Francisco Marathon event that happens every summer. This was the first race I ran since 2019 *without* Anusha and Samyak cheering for me near the finish line. They were in Germany for summer vacation.

It was my first race after starting *Changesmith*.

Considering my business priorities for the year 2023, I decided to forego the Germany trip. With this decision, I became more accountable for business results and I also redoubled the efforts on training. To remind me of this, I had a customized name on the race bib: *Changesmith*.

The training plan included speed drills that were beyond my reach. I trained for four months for this race: April to July. Over time, I felt comfortable running at the required speed in interval runs, although sustaining that speed for 10 kilometers was not guaranteed.

The weather was great on race day—pleasant and breezy. The crowd was energetic and supportive.

I raced my plan and everything worked well till the 7-kilometer mark. After that, I slowed down.

Thoughts of not achieving the goal swarmed in my head. As I noticed those thoughts, I realized I didn't have to believe my thoughts. This was a unique experience in my racing career, being fully aware of my thoughts and realizing their impact on my performance.

In previous races, I succumbed to those thoughts and let them impact racing goals. But this time, I was ready to roll despite their presence. There was a lot at stake this time. I wanted this gritty attitude to overflow into my business goals too. Achieving the goal in this race was a step in the right direction toward getting gritty!

I picked up the pace after the eighth kilometer and finished the race in 44 minutes and 35 seconds!

I was high on energy after the race; one of my best performances since the day I started running. In 2009, my first 10K race took 75 minutes—what a change in 15 years. I shaved off 30 minutes over those years. My fitness level at 43 was better than at age 29—age *is* just a number.

Strong performance and goal achievement in this event injected a new dose of certainty and confidence in my athletic goals.

TIME FOR REFLECTION

- What is your current fitness level, and how does it compare to your ideal level?
- How can you improve further? What can you do this year?

"Whether you think you can, or you think you can't—you're right." - Henry Ford

47

BECOMING A VENDOR AT ORACLE

The third way to generate income for Changesmith is through corporate training and coaching engagements. In this engagement, I work with a group of employees and facilitate a workshop on communication and leadership. A part of this plan is to offer one-on-one coaching to managers in the organizations. I did this for years while being employed at Oracle.

Now it was time to do this as a business owner and full-time leadership coach.

Since I was employed at Oracle for nineteen years, I thought of starting there. I know the culture very well and I'm aware of many organizations that I can approach to offer my services. The first step here was to become a registered vendor in their procurement system.

The biggest benefit of being a vendor at Oracle is this: any team at Oracle can hire me as a coach or workshop facilitator. These engagements are paid by the company's learning and development budget; employees don't pay from their pocket. This is a win-win situation for everyone.

I started with my one-on-one coaching clients who were managers. I found one manager who was keen to conduct a session for her team at Oracle. We went through the vendor onboarding process which took several weeks. I submitted relevant business documents for scrutiny and background checks.

After that, I got an official email from Oracle welcoming me as an approved vendor. This was a moment of pride and satisfaction. Changesmith Coaching is a vendor at Oracle offering leadership coaching programs. I was a business owner offering my services to my previous employer; I loved this!

I first visited the Oracle Redwood Shores campus in the US in 2002 as a software engineer. Twenty-one years later, in July 2023, I visited the campus for a workshop as a facilitator. Life has changed so much. I have grown so much through goals, one goal at a time.

I did two working sessions with one team. It was a hybrid training program. Some attended in person, and a few dialed in remotely from other cities across the US, Mexico, and Romania.

The training was well received. In the anonymous survey I conducted after the sessions, lots of positive remarks came regarding content, delivery, and audience engagement. I was excited like a kid in a candy store! I have so many ideas for workshops and practical ways to help people communicate and collaborate to achieve common goals in the workplace. It was thrilling to see how my ideas impacted the audience.

Becoming a vendor at Oracle has been a significant milestone and social proof for Changesmith Coaching. Many people who attend my cohort-based courses connect me to their learning and development teams. Before they ask me, I know what documents they need to add me as a vendor to their procurement system. It becomes easy for them and I play the game of vendor onboarding like a pro! Let's talk about my cohort courses next.

TIME FOR REFLECTION

- Does your employer offer an internal coaching or mentoring program?
- How can this program assist you? When are you able to sign up?

"I've come to believe that each of us has a personal calling that's as unique as a fingerprint and that the best way to succeed is to discover what you love and then find a way to offer it to others in the form of service, working hard, and also allowing the energy of the universe to lead you." - Oprah Winfrey

The term *oracle* has its origins in ancient Greek. It comes from the Greek word (órama), which means "what is seen or vision." In ancient Greece, an oracle referred to a person or place considered to be a source of divine wisdom or prophecy. One of the most famous oracles was the Oracle of Delphi, where the god Apollo was believed to impart guidance and predictions through priestesses known as Pythias.

48

CREATING COHORT COURSES

B efore formally engaging with clients, I provide two complimentary sessions to potential clients where each session is 60 minutes long. This helps me and the client decide if this is a fruitful engagement. These two sessions act as a filter for client selection—it's a two-way filter. Two trial sessions also allow them to test the process and see if they like working with me.

Between March and August 2023, I provided complimentary coaching sessions to more than 50 people. In the process, I realized the need for other ways of generating income. One-on-one coaching is difficult to scale. It's super fulfilling and rewarding, however, we all have only 24 hours a day, so scaling up is unrealistic.

The immediate thought I had was to consider cohort-based programs. I had done group workshops at Oracle since 2007 and I knew this was an area where I would shine.

With a cohort-based model, I could scale my reach and impact. I would be able to help people from several countries and companies in a group session at once. Online cohort-based courses are a wonderful way to learn new skills. People love it! It's more engaging and impactful than watching recorded training. There are several platforms available today to host live cohort courses.

I did my research and finally decided to host the courses on Maven, which is a popular marketplace for cohort courses.

I designed three courses: *Communication Engineering, Storytelling in the Tech World, and Becoming a Slidesmith.*

My first course, Communication Engineering, was launched on September 18th, 2023. I offered discounted seats and free trials for organizations in my network. *Try before you buy* is a proven way to show the value first. This model works great in cohort courses since the effort doesn't change with the group size.

Initially, 20 percent were paying students and 80 percent were on free trials. Now, it's the other way around, I have 80 percent paying students in my live courses.

As of this writing in 2024, hundreds of people from eleven countries have taken the cohort courses offered by Changesmith.

This is the impact I wanted to have through my personal growth in the last twenty years. Finding another job is easy, but achieving this kind of impact is so fulfilling and enriching. Of course, it's hard work, but the effort is worth its weight in gold. *Work is play here!*

With a sense of pride and satisfaction, I have listed a few companies and countries below.

Companies: Airbnb, Amazon, Meta, Oracle, Microsoft, Fidelity, Google, AT&T, Nvidia, Salesforce, PWC, EY, Nubank, SAP and many more…

Countries: India, Ireland, Mexico, Poland, Hungary, Germany, Canada, Romania, Netherlands, Brazil, and the United States.

The personal growth I experienced through this goal has been transformative. Writing a marketing copy for the course, marketing the course via email and social media, pricing, and selling the course benefits to learning and development teams are critical skills I mastered in this journey as a course creator.

The quote, "If you build it, they will come," rings in my ears when I think about my courses. Practical and transformative courses attract people; I'm glad my courses are helpful. I'm inspired and fulfilled by student reviews of these courses.

TIME FOR REFLECTION

- What skills would you like to build or improve?
- Which cohort-based courses can assist you in elevating your skills?

"Success in business requires training and discipline and hard work. But if you're not frightened by these things, the opportunities are just as great today as they ever were." - David Rockefeller

The word *cohort* traces its origins to ancient Rome. It comes from the Latin word *cohors*, which originally referred to a military unit, specifically a group of approximately 600 soldiers commanded by a tribune. In contemporary English, *cohort* typically denotes a group of people with a shared characteristic, experience, or background, often used in academic, social, or organizational contexts.

49

GETTING FIRST PLACE IN A 10K RACE

In the 2022 San Jose 10K race, I finished in the third position in my category, completing the race in 46 minutes. The first-place finisher completed it in 44 minutes.

With the latest performance, I was now at 44.35 minutes. I thought, "Can I get this to under 44 minutes?" Winning first place was a natural extension of that, but my focus was on yet another strong performance.

I discussed this with my coach. Ash said I could even attempt sub-43, considering my track record and past performance. We settled for a sub-44 goal. The race was in October 2023. I wrote, *"Sub-44 at 44,"* in my journal as an anchor for this goal. I turned 44 a week before this race. Achieving this goal was my gift to myself!

Since I had great confidence and fitness from the race in July, the training was easier this time. I was eager to perform better in each training run, giving my best each time. I noticed my stress levels were low during this time, hence recovery between runs was great.

For the first time in my racing career, I felt fully prepared. I knew for sure I would achieve this goal, without a shadow of a doubt! Such a level of self-efficacy and calmness were new to me. Starting a business as a solopreneur was definitely a factor behind this newfound self-efficacy.

I was in corral number one this time due to a previous race timing of under 45 minutes. I felt like an elite runner right at the frontline with a pack of runners who had all earned the right to be in that corral. It was deeply satisfying. It was a moment to remember—a moment to celebrate and cherish. Anusha and Samyak were thrilled to see me at the front of the start line.

I followed the race plan to the letter. No stress, no pain, and no doubtful thoughts swarming around me this time.

I finished the race in 43 minutes and 36 seconds. As I crossed the finish line, I jumped up with excitement. *"Sub-44 at 44"* was a reality! What was on my mind earlier, was in my hand now—a race medal that symbolized this goal.

As I walked out of the secured area near the finish line, amidst this euphoric moment, Samyak ran to me to show the race results. You guessed right!

I was in first place in my age group. There are no words to describe that feeling. I truly felt like an elite athlete that day—a former *couch potato* who worked for twenty years to become an *athlete*!

On the race day, I was at my peak fitness; I weighed *66.5 kilograms (or 146 pounds)*. If you remember, on the day of writing my first five goals in 2003, I weighed *89 kilograms (or 196 pounds)*.

Throughout this race, I performed like a pro. I knew I had reached a new level of thinking and performance through consistent effort in my quest for excellence in goal achievement.

TIME FOR REFLECTION

- What are your thoughts on pursuing goals that you believe may be beyond your reach? Is there something you feel isn't meant for you?
- If you achieve that goal, how would it change your self-perception?

"It always seems impossible until it's done." - Nelson Mandela

Running a sub-44-minute 10K is considered an elite-level performance, placing the runner among the top competitors in their age group. It requires maintaining an average pace of around seven minutes per mile (or four minutes and 20 seconds per kilometer), showcasing remarkable speed and fitness.

50

ACHIEVING 45 PERCENT OF MY REVENUE GOAL

I had a three-pronged strategy to achieve the revenue goal in the year 2023: one-on-one coaching, cohort courses, and corporate engagements.

Close to 50 percent of the projected revenue hinged on two corporate engagements. These engagements had one-on-one coaching and group training on leadership and communication. Both projects didn't take off due to budget cuts and layoffs in those organizations; they were out of my control.

The planned engagements were canceled at the last minute, like a flight getting canceled due to bad weather while you're waiting to board. It was totally unexpected and it hit the bottom line of Changesmith. I didn't make the income I set out initially. Even though I didn't achieve my goal 100 percent, I was happy and hopeful. Wonder why? I'll tell you.

The company was registered on February 28, 2023, and had positive cash flow within a month. Within nine months, I hit 45 percent of my target. Here's what I thought, "If I could make 45 percent of my goal, I will also be able to hit 100 percent of my goal in the future." It was just a matter of time.

For twenty-one years, I worked in the software industry. I traded time for money for thirteen years in India followed by eight in the United States. Starting a business and making the same income at the drop of a hat is unrealistic. It wasn't a planned move—a purpose-driven move and a passion-driven venture for sure. I was indeed grateful to see this money flow in the first year. It breathed belief in me and kept me going. I had enough data to move forward on my plan.

This experience also humbled me. I realized I needed support. I needed to review my game plan with someone who's been in the business of coaching for a long time and doing it well. There was a clear need for a coach to hold me accountable for my actions, difficult choices, and disciplined work.

A coach needs a coach too. *Coaches don't live in ivory towers.* We are all climbing on a ladder of consciousness. People above us on a higher rung on this ladder can help. Such help can come through a coaching conversation, holding a safe space for vulnerability, finding alternatives, and staying on the path of action.

I signed up for a long-term coaching engagement with Dr. Eric Maisel. Eric has more than 40 years of experience in family therapy and creativity coaching. He's a prolific author with sixty books published so far. Eric also runs creativity seminars and retreats around the world in addition to one-on-one coaching. His profile perfectly matches the picture I have in my mind for the future of Changesmith as a solopreneur.

I'm glad I chose to work with him. We meet once every two weeks for an online coaching session.

Working with Eric, I crafted a new business strategy for the year 2024 and beyond. We came up with a renewed one-on-one coaching engagement model and a marketing plan that can withstand the weather of the economy. I feel confident about this new game plan.

With the setback in the 2023 revenue goal, I became stronger. After experiencing the worst-case scenario, I became calmer. And the business strategy became more coherent and forward-looking.

TIME FOR REFLECTION

- Have you recently fallen short of achieving any of your goals?
- What data did you gather from that experience? How can it help you?

"A setback is a setup for a comeback." - Willie Jolley

51

EXPERIMENTING WITH DIET
AND NUTRITION

As I shared earlier in a previous chapter, I turned vegan in 2019 while training for a marathon. I was a vegetarian before this decision. My definition of a vegetarian diet: plant-based food along with dairy. In 2019, I cut out dairy from my diet. I felt more energetic without it. This experiment was inspired by Brendan Brazier's book *Thrive*.

After four years of eating like this, my routine blood test indicated the onset of a metabolic disorder.

It's not the vegan diet per se, it's how my body responded to the changes I made. My diet became carb-heavy in the absence of dairy to consume adequate protein every day. The changes were made in a hurry without any data or experimentation. It was time to reflect and course-correct.

Some indicators that caused concern were low HDL, low Vitamin D, low Vitamin B12, and elevated levels of triglycerides. This combination can expose us to a host of health issues in the long run.

I decided to become a pro in nutrition by working with an expert. Optimizing health through nutrition became my goal.

I signed up for a 90-day nutrition coaching with Amy Love. She's a retired nurse with over four decades of experience. She's passionate about helping people maintain optimum health through nutrition. In other words, treating food as medicine.

Amy comes from a camp of low-carb diets. There's a lot of research behind a low-carb diet and its benefits on healthspan. The first thing we did was track my diet. Tracking what, when, and how much wasn't easy. While the mobile app was easy to use, the mindset change was not.

Weighing food to see how many grams of rice or vegetables I ate was an additional step before meals. We tracked my intake for three weeks without making any changes; simply noticing what I ate every day. Awareness helps us decide what can be changed. This theme echoes in the world of diet and nutrition too.

Some things emerged from the captured data. I wasn't getting enough healthy fats. My diet was carb-heavy. My lab markers were correlated with my eating habits. She had a clear plan and call to action. I was ready to follow her guidance for the next six months.

Our next step was to run some tests on my body's responses to dietary changes. We increased fat consumption and decreased carbs significantly. I had the goal of consuming 130 grams of fat every day. I have never eaten this amount of fat in my life. I added coconut milk, olive oil, avocados, nuts, and seeds. As an experiment, I also added dairy back to my diet after a gap of four years.

It was difficult to meet my daily fat goal. I felt full and did not have enough space to eat more but I enjoyed experimenting with these changes.

It was interesting to see how to play the nutrition game with food. Before this, I didn't have a good grasp of macronutrients and how many grams of carbohydrates, fat, or protein I was eating every day. With six weeks of food tracking on a mobile app, I learned a lot about various foods and their nutrient composition. I had a clear sense of what I ate in each meal I consumed.

As I became mindful of my choices, I started eating less. Satiety followed me for a longer duration. I wasn't hungry between meals. To elevate my Vitamin D level, I walked in the sun twice a day for 10 minutes. I didn't take any supplements to resolve it. Natural remedies are the best choice.

After 60 days of making changes, we did the required blood tests to see the impact. Good cholesterol increased by 10 points, my Vitamin D number doubled and my triglyceride number slightly lowered. The odd man out was cholesterol. It increased.

It was a time to celebrate. The body was responding to the changes I made. My HDL level was at its highest in a decade! It was a step in the right direction. I saw sunny days ahead of me.

During these two months, I had significantly consumed dairy products. I was ready for the next experiment: decreasing dairy consumption and increasing unsaturated fats in my diet. In this experiment, I removed everything from the dairy family except for ghee (clarified butter). We added a good portion of low-glycemic fruits as well. I reduced my total fat consumption from 130 grams to 100 grams; most of these 100 grams consisted of unsaturated fats.

As of this writing, I'm making sustained progress in this domain. I'll continue to run experiments to optimize my health through proper diet and nutrition. It's more fun to play the game when you know you're making *progress!* Progress excites us to continue playing.

In four decades of my life, I had never been this rigorous about nutrition. It requires great discipline and consistency to follow a nutrition regime. Getting distracted is easy; one meal can spoil a day's plan. A cheat day can stretch into a cheat week or month. Most importantly, patience is key.

It takes several weeks to see changes in body and blood work. Without a goal and constant motivation, it's just a fad. Sustained change is paramount.

If you have never tried pulling levers on your nutrition, I hope this chapter inspires you to attempt it once. Give it a shot and seek an expert's help. You have nothing to lose, but a lot to gain.

TIME FOR REFLECTION

- How is your eating pattern, and have you tracked your diet lately?
- Would you be open to tracking your diet for 30 or 60 days, and how could you ensure you stay committed?

"Let food be thy medicine." - Hippocrates

52

WRITING A BOOK

One item from my list of goals was writing a book. I wrote this goal in 2005 after becoming a confident speaker in the Toastmasters Club. I wanted to share my growth journey with others and help them go beyond their limits through goals.

In October 2023, while talking to Dr. Eric Maisel in a coaching session, I shared this goal. His immediate response was, "Start writing today."

I was zapped. I took a few seconds to collect my thoughts and said, "It's a lot of effort and I'm not ready at this point. I have a lot to take care of right now."

Eric said, "That's just anxiety talking. There's never a good time to start writing your book."

He then gave me three options to choose from: write 20, 40, or 60 minutes every day. I was scared to pick. Not writing wasn't a choice. I would have opted for not writing if it was available. Sheepishly I picked 20 minutes as my goal.

Eric smiled and said, "Most of my clients start with 20 minutes. You made a good choice."

That's the power of a coaching conversation. With a coach, you can explore possibilities and find new pathways for making progress. After the session, I started a daily writing practice.

My first day of writing was tough. I set a timer for 21 minutes; 21 kilometers is the distance of a half marathon. I *love* this number. I wrote random thoughts on why I wanted to write a book and how I started writing one after a coaching session with Eric.

Writing without a structure was difficult. While writing, an insight flashed in my mind. "What if I write in the chronological order of my goals?" There would be a natural flow and structure. I can easily recollect episodes from 2003 until now, from the day I wrote the first five goals.

With a natural flow to follow, writing became easier. I wrote 500 words in my first writing session. The bonus of writing was that I had a clear path to write for the next few weeks. Jog down the memory trail and jot down my thoughts.

Many days I felt the pull to postpone, skip, or procrastinate the writing exercise. Uninvited thoughts visited me and reminded me to take it easy, sometimes even convincing me how worthless my book would be. Thoughts raced, such as "Who would read this book?" "What's special about my goals?" "Why would people buy this book?"

Thoughts have superpowers. You cannot defeat them by wrestling with them. You can neutralize them by noticing them—objectively—and not getting entangled in the web of thoughts. They wither away like flowers when left unattended. They float away like clouds in the sky.

Sticking to my daily writing ritual, I achieved a streak of 120 days. I wrote 48,000 words at roughly 450 to 500 words per session. There was so much raw material collected in those 120 days! After that, it was a matter of rearranging, polishing, and ensuring coherence across chapters.

The writing process is cathartic. Some memories turned green, some faded ones came back, and a few seemingly small incidents in my life were deemed worthy of writing and sharing in my book.

The toughest part of book writing: *deleting what you have written*! The content editor gave feedback on the book's structure, clarity, and coherence. She asked me to remove 15 percent of what I had written, which was 7,000 words, and summarize the same content in 2,000 words.

Removing words initially felt like chopping my fingers. Every word was priceless to me. After two weeks of deliberation, I followed the editor's advice and cleaned up the manuscript. The book was ready for copyediting and then production. The entire process from the first page to publishing took around *nine* months; it was like *birthing* a baby! It came through me, not from me.

This book is my daughter. I have missed having one. While writing the book, I found that daughter here. I hope she goes around the world and inspires people to aim higher and to live a life of meaning, achievement, and fulfillment.

Most importantly, I hope she inspires her brother Samyak to embrace this way of living—a life organized around meaningful goals and brimming with happiness.

Without a goal first in my mind and then on paper, this book wouldn't be born. I learned a lot by writing this book and bringing it to life. I went *beyond my limits* for this book, and the journey was transformative.

Time for reflection

- What are your thoughts on writing a book?
- What if you start writing a book this year?

"There is no greater agony than bearing an untold story inside you." - Maya Angelou

Section 2

A seven-step framework for goal achievement

As I started seeing results on my first five goals, I began noticing a pattern. I made notes on my experience with each goal. These notes helped me reflect and connect the dots in the process. I kept these notes handy to ensure they helped steer me in the right direction.

To get help from experts, I devoured books on goals, happiness, existentialism, positive psychology, and mental fitness. I *applied* what I learned. Some books gave information; some provided validation. They validated my approach to goal achievement.

I have put all those patterns and practical ideas into a seven-step goal achievement framework.

Like I stated at the beginning of this book, the world doesn't need more information. However, I want to show

how we all can achieve our goals with simple and repeatable steps. My objective in this section is to highlight how simple it can be to make progress toward our goals.

Section 1 was all about demonstration, where I narrated my goals in 40,000 words. Section 2, encompassing 4,000 words, focuses on information. A *lot* more demonstration than information!

I sincerely hope this seven-step framework will inspire you to start your journey with expansive goals. These seven steps will help you define your goals and achieve them.

1. Begin with the end in mind.
2. Become accountable.
3. Define milestones.
4. Take one day at a time.
5. Bounce back.
6. Quit strategically.
7. Enjoy the journey.

The next seven chapters will give you a detailed description of these seven steps.

I have included questions for reflection and journaling in these chapters. I recommend investing time in completing these exercises. They deserve your full attention and sincere intention.

Let's dive into the first step next.

1

BEGIN WITH THE END IN MIND

B eginning with the end in mind is sage advice. What do you *really* want? What makes you come *alive*? What gives *meaning* to you? What puts you in a state of *flow*?

We don't get a chance to ponder these questions as we grow up. Life seems robotic when you don't feel alive, when you don't have a sense of wonder for today, and when you don't bring your whole self to daily activities.

We follow followers; people who may be following someone else.

Imagine a 10-kilometer race. You like someone who's running ahead of you. You follow them to match their speed. In a few minutes, you get tired and slow down. You see another person and you would now like to chase and match their speed. You repeat this and slow down again. What if you repeat this throughout the race, chasing other runners one after another?

More than likely you won't finish the race. Even if you do, you'll crawl to the finish line. You cannot follow other people's plans. They may have a plan and they're racing their plans. You need to race yours. This seems common sense in the running parlance. When it comes to life, this is not common practice.

We're bombarded with information on social media. We iconize other people. Comparison brings conformity. You need to define your success criteria. Don't let others define it for you. Like your fingerprints, your goals, values, and definition of meaning are unique to you.

When you follow others' path, you're selling yourself short. You're depriving this world of your contribution. You're blowing out a candle that can give light and light other candles.

It's not easy to have a clear definition in one sitting. That's fine. You first need to accept the ownership of defining your *end*. No one else will. That takes effort, but it's not impossible.

Take a sheet of paper and a pen. Write answers to the questions below. Let answers come naturally. There's no need to force them, and don't criticize what you write. Simply write whatever comes up.

1. What makes you feel alive?
2. If you were to die tomorrow, what regrets would you have?
3. What are you scared of doing?
4. If you had no fear of failure, what would you do?
5. How can you get paid for doing what you love?
6. What are your greatest strengths?
7. What areas of your life need work (health, fitness, finance, relationship, leadership, etc.)?
8. What goals bring meaning to you?
9. What would you like to accomplish in your life?

Sometimes it may take more than a few sessions of writing to come up with clear answers. That's perfectly fine. You can do this several times. You'll find patterns and themes after a while that emerge from your writing. That's how it works. It has worked for me and for hundreds of other people that I have worked with in coaching engagements.

If you have finished writing answers to these questions, *Congratulations!*

You're now in the top 5 percent of people on this planet! You know what you want. That's huge.

Very few people think about this aspect, let alone writing it down. Life is busy. Busyness has become the business of life. It's like driving your car for days with no time to rest or refuel. What's the point? If you don't know where you're going, does speed matter? Distance? Nope.

TIME FOR REFLECTION

- If you repeat the journaling exercise above five times, what common themes would show up?
- What can you learn from those themes?

"Your work is to discover your work and then, with all your heart, to give yourself to it." - Buddha

2

Become accountable

To make progress toward any worthwhile goal, build accountability. We all behave better and perform well with external accountability. I have worked with coaches since 2007. I highly advise you to try it. If you're not ready yet to work with a coach, you can explore other options for accountability: a friend, a family member, or join a community that has high standards. Experiment to choose what works best, and then stick with it.

Many times, in my life, I have seen good intentions not translate into decisive actions. The building plan is on the table, but the building (life) doesn't get built. It stays on paper. Glorified intentions don't bring meaning and happiness, it's the action that does. That's when the rubber meets the road!

When you're looking for a coach, remember this: *Performance = Potential - Interference.* [5]

A coach's job is to help you discover what's interfering in your life: limiting beliefs, stories, or habits.

A coach is not there to share knowledge with you. Knowledge is abundant and free.

We are no longer deprived of information. It's all available now. What's needed is the courage to start and the consistency to finish what we start.

---

5   Timothy Gallwey, *The Inner Game of Tennis* (Random House, 1997)

Your coach may recommend books to read, videos to watch, or courses to explore, but the real value is in coaching conversations. Reflective conversations surface the perceived limits and the invisible glass ceiling. The ceiling is made up of limiting beliefs.

Here's the truth. If we don't attempt, we don't gain anything. If we don't give our best when we can, we will regret it later. The sting of discomfort is nothing compared to the sting of regret, especially the regret at the end of our lives.

The *number one* regret of dying people is, "I wish I'd had the courage to live a life true to myself, not the life others expected of me." [6] Find your true *self*, that's your goal. That goal is personal, it's your potential. It's the acorn that could grow into an oak tree. Your job is to convert this potentiality to actuality. It's the great work of your life. Only you can do it. No one else. And for this to happen, you need an accountability factor.

Coaching conversations bring a new level of awareness and accountability to your life. It's no longer ruled by your habitual mind. Your life becomes a game with conscious choices you make every moment of the day.

When you play this game, with choices that are rooted in your values, there's no need to win. Playing *is* winning. It's an infinite game. The one you get to play every day. You get another chance every single day.

If you decide to work with a coach, be authentic, be vulnerable, and be a person of accountability. Your investment will grow exponentially.

---

6   Bronnie Ware, *The Top Five Regrets of the Dying* (Hay House, 2012)

TIME FOR REFLECTION

- Who can help you as a coach?
- Which friend, family member, or community member can you depend on to hold you accountable for your goals?

"Accountability is the glue that ties commitment to the result."
- Bob Proctor

3

DEFINE MILESTONES

Rome wasn't built in a day. This is true with your life goals as well. Defining meaningful and measurable milestones is a key factor in goal achievement. Without forethought on this aspect, you might abandon your worthy goals in a few weeks. The goal might seem unreachable and intractable. You'll be tripped by your feelings and turn the ship around within days of starting.

If you are planning to run a marathon, your coach will break that goal into milestones (depending on your current fitness and athletic abilities). Shorter races like 5K, 10K, and 21K will be appropriate milestones along the way to a 42-kilometer race. These milestones give you experience, training, and confidence to achieve your ultimate goal.

Many people abandon their goals midway just because they didn't define the right milestones. They stop digging three feet before the gold is found. It's ironic, but true.

Milestones make your goals manageable. We love making progress. We love seeing progress. Milestones are your stepping stones to progress. They are indicators of your effort and efficacy. They inspire you to continue. Success breeds success!

Take your goal to a coach (or journaling session) and reflect on the following prompts:

1. How can I break down this goal into smaller chunks or milestones?
2. What's my strategy to break it down? Time or skill or effort or readiness or others?
3. What's the minimum time needed to test my abilities?
4. On a scale of 1-10, how prepared am I to embark on this journey?
5. Considering my life situation, how much time can I dedicate to this goal every week?
6. What support system do I need to make progress on my journey?
7. Am I ready to give 100 percent to this goal?

As you answer these questions, you'll find yourself getting more clarity on possible milestones and timelines for reaching them. Don't hesitate to write detailed answers. The more you write, the better. Writing is thinking, and thinking is hard.

I hated these writing exercises as a beginner in goal achievement. First, I disliked authors who made me write on paper. Later, I reluctantly wrote the answers without following up with action. After doing this a few times, I realized I didn't want that goal. My desire was low, like a worn magnet that no longer attracts iron filings. It takes a strong desire to make things happen.

Through that realization, I became better at goals. Journaling clarifies your intention.

This is what you'll realize when you start doing these exercises in silence and solitude. In the depth of your consciousness, you know the answers to your questions. You know the solutions to your challenges. You're so busy at the surface level. Take some time to dig deep. You'll find gold.

TIME FOR REFLECTION

- Have you answered the seven questions above?
- Are you ready to make progress on your goals?

"You don't have to see the whole staircase, just take the first step."
- Martin Luther King Jr.

4

TAKE ONE DAY AT A TIME

The number one secret of goal achievement is this: daily incremental progress. This one idea when implemented consistently can create magic in your life.

Time is a great equalizer. Regardless of our backgrounds, skills, and abilities, we all have the same amount of time—24 hours a day.

Our success lies in what we put in these 24 hours. We can fill them with activities that move forward toward our goals or with activities that keep us busy being busy—without making any progress. It's always a choice, a choice that seems invisible, even though it's glaring at us every moment.

Your day is like a brick on a wall. If you focus on the wall in its entirety, you'll be terrified. It feels overwhelming, impractical, and impossible.

Shift your focus to the brick. Your job is to daily lay one brick at a time as mindfully as you can. And repeat this the next day. Over and over and over. Success is found in daily improvements. When you focus on one brick at a time, life becomes easy. You know a brick that's set well today is adding up to something big later. It's a matter of time.

Whatever goals you have on your list, break them down into meaningful milestones. And then define daily activities to make progress, bit by bit, day by day. Guard these daily activities with fierce care like you protect expensive jewelry. Otherwise, distractions will sway you hither and thither, chasing a new shiny object every few weeks.

Your goals are big rocks in your daily time jar. Make space for them. Put them in the jar first, before you put in anything else.

Then you pour other things: gravel, sand, and water. Surprisingly these will fill spaces between these rocks and somehow settle in the jar. They're flexible when big rocks are at the bottom.

Try the other way, first pour gravel, sand, and water, before putting the rocks; you'll be left with no space for big rocks at all. I remember this demonstration by Dr. Stephen Covey in a training video in 2003. It was a moment of epiphany for me—the time jar was a great analogy to internalize this idea which is now tattooed in my consciousness.

I integrated the concept of a time jar into my life. It made a huge impact on my goals. I hope you'll keep this analogy as a reminder of how to plan your day. Nothing comes at the expense of your big rocks. You define the "big rocks" in your day, no one else will do it for you.

Once you define the big rocks, it's liberating. You're no longer a candle in the wind. You're not a cork floating on water. You're a torpedo, continuously moving toward a target—your target.

I have lived my life both ways: as a cork and a torpedo. Hands down, torpedo life is blissful. Goal-oriented life is a combination of achievement and fulfillment.

If you like journaling, you can write your big rocks for the day right after you wake up. They can be based on your medium-to-long-term goals.

If I'm training for a race, one of my big rocks for the day would be to finish my workout before seven in the morning. I would feel the energy rush after my run. I would feel like a winner since I first put the big rocks in the jar. The rest will settle in the jar on their own.

In summary, let's review the two steps to master your day and create masterpiece days!

1. Define your "big rocks" for the day.
2. Prioritize them in your day. Do them as soon as you can. Do not push them later in the day.

We all have high energy during some hours of the day. Find your high-energy window. Do your most important work (a.k.a big rocks) in this window. With this strategy applied consistently, you'll make daily progress on your goals. Each day will be a perfect brick on the wall.

Remember, your focus is one brick at a time. Do it with intention and attention. Over time, you'll see a well-built wall. The wall of goals of your life! A wall filled with your meaningful achievements and deep fulfillment! We all deserve and desire that wall. We can build that wall one brick at a time, one day at a time.

TIME FOR REFLECTION

- What can change in your daily routine to accommodate your goals?
- What can be deleted from your routine to make your day more productive?

"You will never change your life until you change something you do daily. The secret of your success is found in your daily routine."
- John C. Maxwell

5

BOUNCE BACK

L ife throws curveballs at everyone. No matter how well we plan, we are always going to have surprises. What differentiates pros from beginners in goals? Pros know this will happen. They anticipate this and have a clear plan for bouncing back, coming out stronger on the other side.

Life can take unexpected turns: a job loss, a loss in the family, health challenges, or financial setbacks. Challenges in life are like resistance training, they build resilience muscles. Weak muscles in one area may affect or impact other areas. For example, your first marathon plan may need to be revisited if you have health challenges or lose your job due to downsizing. I'm not saying it has to, but it's prudent to be open to this possibility.

When you're not open, you're in denial and that will decrease your overall life satisfaction. It's a test of your persistence. You may take a detour or pause, but you don't need to stop.

The most common mistake I have seen people make is this: not acknowledging that we have a situation to address. People turn a blind eye to problems and continue pushing through their goals. This is like trying to blow out an electric bulb; it's wasted effort. Contrary to popular opinion, this will fire back.

I have personally experienced this. When I was planning to sign up for a marathon, I had already run several half marathons. I experienced severe calf pain on long runs after two hours of running. My physiotherapist recommended postponing the marathon goal. I followed his advice. It was the right decision at the time. I would have injured myself otherwise due to overtraining. So, the first step is acknowledging challenges and making changes to your goal.

Once you decide to make changes to your goal by changing time, intensity, or defining subgoals, you gain clarity on what to pursue instead of the original goal.

In my case, I continued to be fit through non-running workouts and weight training. My focus shifted toward recovery, building aerobic capacity, and increasing flexibility. I continued to prepare for the marathon goal, doing the basic work needed until I was ready for a longer race. With this plan, I was still making progress, small and steady, slowly getting ready for a bigger milestone.

As you do this, keep an eye on the best time to bounce back to the original path. The path patiently waits for you. It doesn't go anywhere. You are the one who stepped off for a reason. When you go back on the path, the path will welcome you with open arms. You can start where you left off.

Develop a ramp-up plan so that you don't get flustered with increased commitment when you bounce back. It's like loading the weight incrementally while doing bench presses.

Mastering this bounce-back process is a critical skill in goal achievement. You need to accept it and above all, expect this to happen.

It happens to everyone. Remember: it's a test. You can pause and plan to respond well during the slowdown. In a matter of time, you'll be back in the arena chasing your goal.

TIME FOR REFLECTION

- Are you currently on a detour? If yes, do you have a ramp-up plan?
- How can you continue to make tiny progress during this downtime?

"Life is not about how fast you run or how high you climb, but how well you bounce." - Vivian Komori

6

Quit strategically

Winners never quit. This seems to be a mantra for people who are determined to accomplish their goals no matter what. Turns out, this is unwise. There are some situations where you may need to let go of your goals, perhaps because they're too expensive, they affect other areas of your life, or take too much of your time at the expense of other priorities.

Life is a buffet filled with experiences. You might not enjoy eating only desserts to replace a meal!

Does it mean you can quit all the time? No, certainly not. That's not what I'm saying. That's called "serial quitting," which is simply stopping everything we start and finding the next shiny goal to follow. In Sanskrit, there's a word *Arambhashura*, which means, "hero at the beginning"— someone who tiptoes out the backdoor after starting a new affair with a fanfare of trumpets.

That's immature and childish. I'm asking you to embrace "strategic quitting." This means you consider all your options and gracefully exit the race, knowing you're not ready to invest more energy in the pursuit anymore.

With strategic quitting, you have a team to support you: your coach, family, and close friends. They are by your side to review what's at stake and tell you the truth. They know you'll fail even when you achieve the goal. This is particularly true for goals that affect your relationships.

If you're faced with such a situation, go back to your *why*. Reflect on the importance of your goal relative to the larger goals of your life. Would you regret missing this goal? Or would you regret achieving this goal at the expense of other goals? When in doubt, write things out—on paper.

We all have a finite amount of time and energy. Invest them in the best projects of your life. You need to be ruthless in prioritizing. And be ready to let go of small gemstones to focus on grand diamonds in your life.

You can enlist support from your coach, mentor, or a family member to discuss your plan and arrive at a decision. If you still want to persist, go ahead. You have done the analysis and you know you're minimizing regrets in your life. So, go ahead. Good luck and Godspeed.

However, if you decide to exit gracefully, stop pursuing the goal. It may hurt temporarily, but it's a wise decision in the long run. The key is to find other goals to keep yourself focused and productive.

Life is an adventure. You could do so many things. The sky's the limit, so find something else that piques your interest and passion and put that on your list. Or pick a new item from your goal list, if you have one!

TIME FOR REFLECTION

- How do you know when to quit strategically?
- Who can support you to be objective when making this decision?

"You have to know when to quit. Know when to walk away. When the time comes, it's not going to be easy, but you have to do it for yourself." - Unknown

7

ENJOY THE JOURNEY

The journey is more important than the destination. A mountaineer enjoys the experience of climbing. Reaching the top is a metaphor, but the real benefit is the experience of climbing toward the peak. It's not what you do, it's what you "become" in the process of goal achievement that matters. This has been a recurring theme in my journey with goals for more than twenty years.

Some goals transform you from a caterpillar into a butterfly. If you look back at your life, you'll find at least one goal that transformed you—a goal that changed your beliefs, outlook, and self-concept. I have cited several examples from my personal experience in this book.

With so much at stake, what if you dread the process? What if you agonize over the effort? Quibble over consistent work? It seems odd. It's like complaining about the hole in the doughnut. The doughnut comes with a hole; it's by design. It's not a defect, it's a feature.

I'll admit to moaning about effort. I did it initially, and I see many people falling into this quicksand of victimhood—especially when the going gets tough!

You need to remember two words on your journey: *graceful* and *grateful*.

Graceful: You're likely to enjoy the process with grace. Being graceful is not our instinct. We groan while doing difficult (or what we perceive as difficult) things. We moan, complain, and push through them.

A pro would shun this. A pro would be graceful in difficult times. A pro would not behave like an amateur letting their feelings get the better of them. Showing frustration, irritation, or acting on impulses are examples of not being graceful.

Grateful: Some of your goals are going to be demanding. They'll ask for a time-slice from your loved ones, support from friends and family, or deeper involvement of your coach. It takes a village to raise a child; it takes a team to support your goals. So be grateful for whatever support you're getting along the way. If you're up for it, get drunk on gratitude.

Openly express your gratitude; the more frequently the better. Start with your inner circle (immediate family). Their support is like the wind on your back. You need it. We all need it. I'm truly grateful to my wife Anusha for her encouragement and support as a partner. She has been a pillar of support in pursuit of my expansive goals. The journey has been joyful.

If you're not having fun on your journey, you're messing it up. You're missing something.

Revisit your purpose and approach. One of them needs tuning. If you're not "in joy," you won't "enjoy." And it's palpable. You'll notice it and others will too—like a drop of bird poop on your shoulder. It smells. You can smell it. Everyone can smell and see it.

You might ask, "What about fear? What if I am afraid of doing something?"

Fear is nothing but thought. Thoughts and feelings are like two sides of a coin. We feel our thoughts every moment. Fear doesn't tell us anything about external events. It's a reflection of your thinking—internal chatter, confusion, and limiting thoughts.

"Do the thing and you shall have the power," Ralph Waldo Emerson quipped.

It's true. We do things first and then experience the power. Wood first, heat next. You cannot sit in front of the fire and yell, "Give me heat first, then I'll add the wood." That would be illogical.

It's like me *demanding* to be "confident" in public speaking before actually speaking. Confidence comes by doing, facing fears, and taking the journey.

You need to put your work first to reap the benefits. One of the benefits is personal power—a level of calm confidence that you have never experienced before.

TIME FOR REFLECTION

• How can you enjoy the journey?
• What if you focus more on the process? How would that help you achieve your goals?

"Success is a journey, not a destination. The doing is often more important than the outcome." - Arthur Ashe

SECTION 3

TOP THREE SABOTEURS OF GOAL ACHIEVEMENT

I have coached hundreds of people in my coaching career. Throughout this journey, I noticed several recurring challenges during client conversations about goal discovery and achievement. These clients wanted to embrace goal-oriented lives, but for some reason could not make meaningful progress.

I would love to be your coach and support you on your journey. That may not be realistic due to time constraints. One-on-one coaching is hard to scale, which is why books are written.

This book is your companion. It has all you need to start your journey. If you still need a coach for a few months, go for it. When you work with a coach, your personal growth will reach a new level in a few months.

Working with a coach is the highest form of personal change. It's a crucible for removing dross from your thinking. Each conversation will remove dirt and unwanted elements from your psyche. You have skin in the game when you work with a coach and high accountability for taking action between sessions.

The next three chapters will describe the top three challenges I have noticed in my clients. Some of these challenges have also troubled me on my journey. I bring two perspectives here, my own experience and witnessing my clients' growth and transformation through these challenges.

Here's the good news, there's light at the end of the tunnel. You just need to keep walking, knowing where you're going and why you're going there.

Once we name these saboteurs, we can tame them; we can claim victory over them!

Let's face these top three saboteurs next.

1

LACK OF PURPOSE

During the initial sessions of a coaching engagement, my clients go through a few reflective exercises to elevate their self-knowledge, to know why they do what they do and why they want what they want. You can find one of those journaling exercises in this chapter.

There are nine questions in this exercise. You can write in a notepad, an online document, or record your answers as a voice memo. You choose your way.

But this is a prerequisite for the next steps in our engagement. A significant number of people have a tough time with this exercise. They come with one of these two situations for the next coaching session.

1) A blank page. They say, "I did my best. I couldn't write anything. I kept scratching off whatever I wrote."

2) Half-baked answers scribbled in small letters. They don't have ownership of what they wrote. They share it with a tone of frustration, "I don't think I can own what I wrote. These are random thoughts. I'm not at all passionate about what I wrote here. Looks like I ticked the box by writing. I'm not committed to what I wrote."

A tough coach would say, "What's stopping you? Fear? Or Laziness?"

I would gently ask you, "What would you do if you had no fear? What would you do if you weren't afraid to fail? What's worth doing even if you fail?"

If that doesn't help you, I'll ask this, "What brings joy to you?" That's the path you need to walk. *Follow your bliss; joy is your compass.*

Some people also say, "I don't know my life purpose." As if your life has just one purpose, either you know it or don't. As if it's binary, zero or one, nothing in between.

That's a fallacy. Our life can have multiple purposes.

Meaning and happiness are the indicators. Whatever gives you meaning or happiness, could be one of your purposes. For instance, every time I donate blood, I find both meaning and happiness. It's one of my purposes. I cannot say it's the purpose of my life. That would be too narrow. I have so many other things that sprinkle meaning in my life salad. So do you.

You don't have to latch on to one *big* purpose. There's no big or small when it comes to your purpose. Size doesn't matter, but presence does.

If you struggle to come up with a list of your goals, try an alternative. Focus on living your day fully invested in your values. If you value health and well-being, do something every day toward your health. Follow tiny steps consistently. Demonstrate your values in your daily choices—small and big. Of course, for this, you need to be aware of your values first so you can demonstrate them in your choices.

While you live based on your values, along the way you'll discover your life purposes. A common pattern will emerge like a Polaroid picture slowly emerging after a few minutes. Be patient. Be fully engaged in your life. Be observant in finding patterns and themes.

One last piece of advice: you are welcome to do this journaling exercise *several* times. That's another way to find themes and patterns around what matters to you.

Choose your way: notepad, online doc, or voice recorder.

It's like building muscles. Would you build muscles by watching dumbbells every day? *No.* You would build them by lifting dumbbells, many reps, over and over. Your body will overcompensate by growing muscle as the muscle fibers break down during exercise.

The same rule applies here. Let those fibers break, let your purpose muscle be built via reps. The more, the better.

The outcome? Strong purpose muscles that'll lift heavy goals in your life!

Nine journaling questions:

1. What are you most passionate about?
2. What are your greatest strengths?
3. How can you get paid for doing what you love?
4. When do you feel most alive? What circumstances? Around what people?
5. What were your five greatest accomplishments over the last five years?
6. What will your five greatest accomplishments be over the next five years? Then twenty-five years?
7. How can you best share your gift with the world?
8. What would you do if you were not afraid?
9. If you were guaranteed to succeed, what would you dare to do?

TIME FOR REFLECTION

- Have you completed the journaling exercise above?
- If not, what's stopping you? Please invest time and answer these nine questions.

"Life has no meaning. Each of us has meaning and we bring it to life. It is a waste to be asking the question when you are the answer." - Dr. Joseph Campbell

2

LACK OF TIME

My grandfather was an elementary school teacher for over three decades. He had two favorite quotes. One, "Time and tide wait for none." Two, "Early to bed and early to rise makes you healthy, wealthy, and wise."

He embodied these two quotes. I watched him for twenty years. He led a life that exemplified them. Over the years, I have found both quotes practical and helpful.

Time levels the playing field. We all get the same 24 hours in a day—no more, no less, exactly 24 hours. What separates people with and without fulfillment is how we invest those hours—16 waking hours every day (I hope you're sleeping well in the remaining eight hours). We can invest an hour or spend an hour. It depends on the activity. You get to decide and you need to own your decision.

A common theme that comes up in coaching is "I don't have time" or "I'm too busy."

In most cases, it comes to not knowing what's important, the inability to distinguish between urgent and important tasks and then relentlessly prioritizing "important" tasks first or creating time blocks for them.

In my journey, I have seen three levels of time management. These levels are cumulative. Level 3 includes skills from 2 and 1. Level 2 includes Level 1 skills.

Level 1 is about creating blocks of time for important tasks. Many people struggle here. Mindless distractions and lack of self-awareness steal time. At this level, people can carve out time for what they want to achieve. For many, this is a dream come true. If you're not at this level, this is the first rung of the ladder to be on.

Level 2 is energy management. Here you can carve out time and show up with full energy to get your stuff accomplished. Energy—physical, mental, and emotional—is paramount. At this level, you have well-nurtured habits to generate and maintain the energy required to accomplish your goals.

Level 3 is all about attention management. Here, you can focus your attention on one thing for a chosen duration. Like a magnifying glass burning a dry leaf, you're burning away the task by making progress and reducing its size. Internal chatter is silenced; impulses are in control. You're in flow and you're moving forward. Like a bullet train going at full speed toward its destination. Nothing can hinder or stop you.

If you're facing difficulties in time management, start with time tracking. Simply observe how you spend or invest your waking hours for a week. Track what you do every hour. This log tells you the truth. It won't please you, but will surely serve you. You'll see the truth like daylight—the whole truth, nothing but the truth. You'll know where you are on the ladder of time management.

I would like to offer five practical tips to overcome this hurdle of time management.

1. Schedule your screen time, as opposed to unfettered access to your phone during your working hours.
2. Consider a 12-hour digital fast. You could stay away from electronic devices from 8:00 p.m. to 8:00 a.m. (or 7:00 p.m. to 7:00 a.m.).

3. Revisit your goals to see if they have the required amount of desire and fire to stay focused. A higher desire toward your goals lowers your desire for distractions.

4. Form a ritual to take a break after every 90 minutes of work; get up from your seat and walk around for 5 to 10 minutes.

5. Find an accountability partner to show your time log and commit to making changes to your work habits. Work with someone who wants to change, so you can help each other.

I love this quote from *The Mahabharata* (legendary Indian epic in Sanskrit) below—Devanagari script, transliteration followed by its translation in English.

अहन्यहनि भूतानि गच्छन्ति इह यमालयम् ।
शेषाः स्थावरमिच्छन्ति किमाश्चर्यम् अतः परम् ॥

ahanyahani bhūtāni gacchanti iha yamālayam |
śe⬚ā⬚ sthāvaramicchanti kimāścaryam ata: param ||

In spite of knowing that many living beings die every day, survivors wish to live forever. What can be more astonishing than this?

Perhaps meditating on our mortality is helpful for some people. However, I prefer the other way, a way of reflection.

Reflecting on our dreams, desires, and life goals is a better approach in my experience. This reflection inspires us to consider the hourglass of life and focus on what truly matters.

TIME FOR REFLECTION

- Do you track your time, and if so, at which level would you classify yourself (Level 1, 2, or 3)?
- What changes can you implement to reach Level 3 on the time management ladder?

"The key is not to prioritize what's on your schedule, but to schedule your priorities." - Stephen Covey

3

LACK OF BELIEF

What happens when you grow a pumpkin in a jug? Its growth is stunted. The pumpkin may even look like a jug. The jug is our mind, our habitual thoughts. Pumpkin is what we manifest in life through self-expression. Our minds shape our life experiences, habits, and what we create while we live on this planet.

The mind-jug is made up of beliefs. *Beliefs are repeated thoughts*. We don't see these limiting beliefs. They're like viruses in the air. They affect us and we don't see their presence.

Our childhood experiences play a vital role in forming beliefs. There's so much mud we gather on our psyche— our true self is covered with loads of mud. Lack of belief in ourselves stems from layers of mud leading to powerlessness and hopelessness. When we don't believe, we don't even *attempt* to achieve. That's the power of belief!

All of this happens through our thoughts, and we don't even realize it. Author and motivational speaker Denis Waitley wrote the poem *My Robot R-U-ME2* to describe the phenomenon of our minds controlling our destinies. It's chaotic when the little robot gets out of hand.

I love his poem below. [7]

---

7   Denis Waitley, *Seeds of Greatness* (PocketBooks, 2010)

I have a little robot that goes around with me,
I tell it what I am thinking, I tell it what I see.
I tell my little robot all my hopes and fears,
It listens and remembers everything it hears.
At first, my little robot followed my command,
But after years of training, it's gotten out of hand.
It does not care what's right or wrong, or what is false or true,
No matter what I try now, it tells me what to do.

Thought awareness is not taught in schools and universities. We're on our own on this quest. No one teaches you a course on *Thought 101*.

A belief is a cable wrought with millions of tiny wires called thoughts. It took a long time for me to figure this out through reading, reflecting, meditating, and observing.

I'm *not* my thoughts. I *have* thoughts. I don't need to *think* about my thoughts. I don't need to *believe* all my thoughts. I can notice, witness, and let them go like passing clouds in the sky.

We have a choice to board a train of thought. If a thought doesn't serve you, you can choose not to board that train. It'll go without you. You can build this awareness one day at a time, one thought at a time. That awareness will set you free.

You can start with any reflective practice to fan the flame of awareness: meditation, journaling, breathwork, or just sitting in silence noticing your thoughts. Since 2014, I have been meditating twice a day, 11 minutes per session to kindle this awareness, being the observer of my floating thoughts.

Awareness is like bright light. When you switch on the light, disempowering thoughts disappear like cockroaches skittering away into the dark.

We can then bolster belief through action. You can form a new identity through repeated behaviors.

Identity is nothing but repeated *beingness*. You continue to behave in a new way for a few weeks, you form a new identity.

Our identity comes first, then behaviors, and then feelings. If we let our feelings dictate our behaviors, we're in trouble. By not behaving and taking action, we reinforce a suboptimal identity—a person who's timid, scared, and afraid of taking action.

Create a new *identity* through behaviors. Digging the past doesn't help.

Find out areas of your life that are controlled by negative beliefs through reflective practice. Start challenging them by taking action in alignment with the new identity.

I have seen hundreds of smart, talented, and well-educated people who suffer from a lack of belief. They have a very small sense of self-efficacy. A strong magnet can levitate an object that is up to ten times its weight. Without the magnetic power, a magnet is nothing but a piece of metal. It doesn't levitate anything. Self-belief is the power behind goal achievement; it drives our behaviors.

It's our primary responsibility to get this area sorted out. Whether you have challenges with beliefs or you want to get them back (after a setback), prioritize this. It makes a sea of difference in your life. Remember: you can breathe belief in yourself through awareness and action!

TIME FOR REFLECTION

- Do you engage in reflection exercises?
- What can you do to increase your awareness through reading, reflecting, meditating, or observing?

"Our deepest fear is not that we are inadequate. Our deepest fear is that we are powerful beyond measure. It is our light, not our darkness that most frightens us. We ask ourselves, 'Who am I to be brilliant, gorgeous, talented, fabulous?' Actually, who are you not to be? You are a child of God. Your playing small does not serve the world. There is nothing enlightened about shrinking so that other people won't feel insecure around you. We are all meant to shine, as children do. We were born to manifest the glory of God that is within us. It's not just in some of us; it's in everyone. And as we let our own light shine, we unconsciously give other people permission to do the same. As we are liberated from our own fear, our presence automatically liberates others."
- Marianne Williamson

CONCLUSION

As I write this chapter, I am filled with wonder and gratitude: wonder because I *wrote* this book, gratitude because I wrote it as a *goal* on my list. Without that goal, this book wouldn't have come alive. It would have remained as a seed that never sprouted. John Goddard inspired me in the year 2003. He showed what's possible through his life. John didn't preach or try to persuade me to set goals. He led by example. That's what we need in today's world—a personal example to move from information to implementation.

"Now is the time to get serious about living your ideals. Once you have determined the spiritual principles you wish to exemplify, abide by these rules as if they were laws, as if it were indeed sinful to compromise them. Don't mind if others don't share your convictions. How long can you afford to put off who you want to be? Your nobler self cannot wait any longer. Put your principles into practice—now. Stop the excuses and the procrastination. This is your life! You aren't a child anymore. The sooner you set yourself to your spiritual program, the happier you will be. The longer you wait, the more you will be vulnerable to mediocrity and feel filled with shame and regret, because you know you are capable of better. From this instant on, vow to stop disappointing yourself. Separate yourself from the mob. Decide to be extraordinary and do what you need to do—now." - Epictetus [8]

You don't need to impress others with your goals. Your goals need not be grand, adventurous, or audacious. They

---

8   Robert Dobbin (Translator), *Epictetus: Discourses and Selected Writings* (Penguin Classics, 2008)

just need to be meaningful to *you*. They should push *you* beyond your limits, challenge *you*, and put *you* in the process of change and growth. You get to define the "true north" for your life, no one else does. Inspiring others is a byproduct.

The moment you work on a goal and invest consistent and persistent effort, you're inspiring people around you. I have seen this effect for twenty-plus years. Our inspired action rubs on other people, like a piece of iron being magnetized. Let nature work its wonders. You simply follow your path. This is the mark of a true leader. Be the exemplar. Embody the wisdom of a warrior, rather than merely cataloging theories on living a good life like a librarian. I was a *librarian* for a long time and I know the difference of being in warrior mode, moving from knowing to doing.

When I started writing this book, I doubted myself. I wondered what difference my story could make. Luckily, I know that this type of limited thinking is simply "passing thoughts." It's best not to engage with them or entertain them as special guests. Taking action would be more useful.

I hope you have enjoyed reading this book. I sincerely hope you challenge yourself to identify your life goals. Once you write them, follow the seven-step framework I have laid out to achieve your goals. When you do it for one goal, you have learned the fundamentals of achieving goals. Then you go for the next one on your list. This is a repeatable framework.

One thing I know for sure. You're not the same person you were when you started this book. You have ascended the ladder of consciousness, reaching a new level of inspired thinking.

If you ever go down the ladder of consciousness, read this book again. Mark your favorite chapters and revisit them to uplift your spirit and enthusiasm.

Remember, you're the hero in your life. You're on a journey. This book is your guide. I'm rooting for you. Your family, friends, and I are waiting for you to start the journey.

Would you take the first step on your journey? I hope you do. I would love to see you accomplish your goals. I wish to meet you someday and hear your stories.

See you soon hero. Go *beyond your limits!*

"Don't aim at success—the more you aim at it and make it a target, the more you are going to miss it. For success, like happiness, cannot be pursued; it must ensue, and it only does so as the unintended side effect of one's personal dedication to a cause greater than oneself or as the by-product of one's surrender to a person other than oneself.

Happiness must happen, and the same holds for success: you have to let it happen by not caring about it. I want you to listen to what your conscience commands you to do and go on to carry it out to the best of your knowledge. Then you will live to see that in the long-run—in the long-run, I say!—success will follow you precisely because you had forgotten to think about it." - Viktor Frankl [9]

---

9   Viktor Frankl, *Man's Search for Meaning* (Pocket, 1997)

Acknowledgments

I want to express my heartfelt appreciation to the following:

- John Goddard for the inspiration offered.
- Toastmasters International for the platform.
- Stephen Covey for the 7 Habits.
- Ian Faria for the introduction of coaching.
- Dr. Marshall Goldsmith for the book *What Got You Here Won't Get You There*.
- Ram Ramanathan for the coach training.
- Tony Robbins for the fire walk.
- J Krishnamurthy for the wisdom provided.
- S. N. Goenka for Vipassana meditation.
- Ash Nath for marathon coaching.
- Bence Gazdag for executive sponsorship.
- Brian Johnson for the Heroic Coach training.
- Dr. Eric Maisel for coaching.
- Thomas Sterner for thought awareness training.
- Scott Allan for mentoring.
- Larry Ellison for Oracle Corporation.
- Mark Zuckerberg for Meta.
- Nassar Stoertz for being the first coaching client in the United States.
- All my coaching clients, cohort students, and workshop participants since 2007 for engagement.
- All my peers, stakeholders, and cross-functional partners at Oracle and Meta for collaborative work. There are too many to name here, so I won't attempt to do so.
- All my mentors, supporters, and cheerleaders who played a role in achieving my goals.

- Umang Vanjara, Krishna Kiran, and Santosh Vijay for giving me early feedback on the manuscript.

Recommended
Reading

I recommend specific books to my clients depending on where they are in their personal evolution and what they need to achieve their goals.

Since this is a book about goals, I will mention six books that provide scientific evidence on the approach and the benefits of goal-based living. These books cover both the *why* and the *how* of goals, as well as how goals intersect with progress, happiness, and meaning.

1. *Succeed* by Heidi Grant Halvorson
2. *The How of Happiness* by Sonja Lyubomirsky
3. *The Happiness Hypothesis* by Jonathan Haidt
4. *One Small Step Can Change Your Life: The Kaizen Way* by Dr. Robert Maurer
5. *Man's Search for Meaning* by Viktor Frankl
6. *Areté* by Brian Johnson

Author's Bio

Pramoda Vyasarao holds a master's degree in computer science. Prior to establishing *Changesmith Coaching LLC*, he amassed 21 years of invaluable experience within technology giants such as Oracle and Meta, both in India and the United States. Commencing his career as an engineer, he swiftly developed a keen interest in personal development, initiating a Toastmasters club for Oracle employees during his tenure. After six years of excelling as an individual contributor, Pramoda transitioned horizontally into management.

During his tenure at Oracle, while overseeing a sizable organization, Pramoda recognized a critical gap in structured leadership development programs. Motivated by this observation, he embarked on a journey of self-improvement, enrolling in several leadership coaching programs as a client. Through dedicated effort and conscious transformation, he experienced a profound shift in his behaviors and beliefs. This personal evolution served as the catalyst for his decision to pursue coach certification programs, with the aim of aiding senior engineers and managers on their own paths to growth.

With 17 years of coaching and workshop facilitation under his belt, Pramoda has left an indelible impact on thousands of individuals across 10 different countries. Within the Changesmith framework, he provides tailored one-on-one coaching for senior leaders, alongside conducting cohort-based courses focusing on communication, leadership, and storytelling. These offerings have garnered significant acclaim, particularly his cohort courses, which enjoy widespread popularity on platforms like Maven.com.

Residing in the vibrant San Francisco Bay Area of California, Pramoda shares his life with his beloved wife Anusha, spirited son Samyak, and their enduring Sulcata companion, Taco.

You can reach Pramoda at https://www.changesmith.me

URGENT PLEA!

Thank You for Reading My Book!
I appreciate all of your feedback and
I love hearing what you have to say.
I need your input to make the next version of this
book and my future books better.

Please take two minutes now to leave a helpful review on
Amazon let me know what you thought of the book:
changesmith.me/book-review

Thanks so much!
- Pramoda Vyasarao